21 Soulful Leade[...] From Motown Hits

MW00333578

LEADERSHIP
SOUL

KENDALL C. WRIGHT
"The Actualizer"

emerge
publishing

26 25 24 23 22 21   1 2 3 4 5 6 7 8 9

LEADERSHIP SOUL

Published by:
Emerge Publishing, LLC
2109 E. 69th Street Tulsa, Oklahoma 74136

Phone: 888.407.4447 www.emerge.pub

Library of Congress Cataloging-in-Publication Data:

ISBN: 978-1-954966-07-9 Trade Paperback
E-book available exclusively on Kindle at www.Amazon.com

BISAC:

BUS019000   BUSINESS & ECONOMICS / Decision-Making & Problem Solving
BUS085000   BUSINESS & ECONOMICS / Organizational Behavior
MUS039000   MUSIC / Genres & Styles / Soul & R 'n B

Printed in the United States of America

Praise for Leadership Soul

"Kendall C. Wright's, *Leadership Soul: 21 Soulful Leadership Lessons From Motown Hits* has made my leadership 'playlist.' As a leadership authority and practitioner for more than three decades, I've seen leadership fluff presented as the real thing. Not this time. This book dives deep, straight to the 'soul' of proven, foundational leadership principles. Read *Leadership Soul,* and you're sure to enjoy some great musical memories, plus you'll be better prepared for the rest of your leadership journey."

Phillip Van Hooser, MBA, CSP, CPAE
Author of *Leaders Ought To Know: 11 Ground Rules for Common Sense Leadership*
Cavett Award recipient

"Delightful, effective, thought provoking! I found myself highlighting wonderful words of wisdom that I wanted to share"

This book will not only have you examining your own leadership style, but also identifying areas in your own organization where these attributes are being displayed. A MUST READ. A great resource! I am currently in an organization that is going through challenges, this book is a game changer!

Celeste R. Didlick-Davis, JD, MS, CFLE
PhD. Educational Leadership ~Miami University

Leadership Soul is a special contribution to moving organizations forward. Kendall C. Wright has spent his professional career studying and assisting leaders seeking to be more effective. In my 31 years as a non-profit CEO and 34 years as a trustee, including 12 as board chair, I've encountered few books that rival the cohesive and visionary book in your hands.

Dwight L. Wilson
Retired, Former General Secretary of Friends General Conference, the oldest American denomination among The Religious Society of Friends

"I love Motown, and I love Kendall C. Wright. And this combination has come together to make you the best leader you will ever be. Kendall is the Master of Motivation. He is a Learned Leader. And he is one of the finest teachers, presenters, and trainers I have ever had the privilege to work with.

In Leadership Soul, Kendall has presented his leadership wisdom in a creative way that will make you sing along as you remember the wonderful music from our past. 5But don't be deceived, it's not your imagination, and you didn't hear it from the g6rapevine.... Baby, this book is for Real!"

Maria Arcocha White
Founder and CEO
Inclusity, LLC

In Leadership Soul: 21 Soulful Leadership Lessons From Motown Hits, Kendall Wright provides an invaluable resource for anyone involved in developing and practicing effective leadership. As a former HR executive and consultant, I regard Leadership Soul as a must-read source of insight that will help stem the *crisis in leadership* tide many observers have noted.

Chip Henderson
HR executive, consultant, educator, continuous learner

"I first meet Kendall in 2006, when I was at Goldman Sachs. He was delivering a series of workshops, and I was his GS Learning & Development 'Sponsor & Host.' To this day, I talk to people about the impact he had on me, and he remains one of the most amazing and engaging facilitators I have had the privilege to meet and work with. The magic he weaved in delivering those workshops and the impact it had, was profound. And that's what makes this book different! This is not another leadership book; this is THE Leadership book! Leadership is not always just about leading others. First, you have to lead yourself. The innovative and anecdotal way he has gone about capturing what that looks like doesn't surprise me; what surprised me reading this book was that I still have so much to learn. The world needs us to lead right now. We all need to read this."

David A Hopley OBE
Director
David Hopley Associates Ltd

"Kendall C. Wright expertly presents, Leadership Soul: 21 Soulful Leadership Lessons From Motown Hits, by uniquely blending the best of Motown title hits into a must-read for any new or existing leader wanting to develop self-awareness and leadership effectiveness. He illustrates the process of self-discovery for leaders and provides a proven pathway for those seeking to develop themselves, individual team members, and creating a more inclusive and effective workplace. Put this book at the top of your reading list."

Greg Jenkins
Greg Jenkins Consulting LLC

In eulogizing his friend, Sandy F. Ray, the inimitable Gardner C. Taylor said, "At the height of his pulpit oratory, it was hard to tell whether one heard music half spoken, or speech half sung." In *Leadership Soul*, my friend Kendall C. Wright has deposited leadership principles within the framework of *Motown melodies* resulting in his book simultaneously speaking and singing! People learn best through means they most enjoy. If you enjoy soul music and want to enjoy learning about leadership rather than merely enduring leadership lessons, then this masterful work is not simply a luxury for you, it is a necessity.

Dr. Robert Smith, Jr.
Charles T. Carter Baptist Chair of Divinity
Beeson Divinity School
Samford University

Whether surfing the web, browsing the stacks of a library, or spending a leisurely afternoon at your local bookstore, it is not a difficult task to find a book on "leadership." A google search for "leadership books" will yield over 858,000,000 options. Rather than having to sift your way through countless books until you find the "one in 858 million" that provides you with the information and insight you need to be a great leader, allow me to recommend *Leadership Soul: 21 Soulful Leadership Lessons From Motown Hits*. Kendall C. Wright, "The Actualizer" has taken his—and our—love for "The Motown Sound" and used it as a foundation to teach important leadership principles. Rather than present a "To Do List" on how to be a great leader, Mr. Wright uses songs that we love, lyrics that we know and artists that we admire to teach impactful lessons that will serve us both personally and professionally. *Leadership Soul* should be on the bookshelf of every leader who is committed to "staying on beat" with the demands of today's ever-changing workplace.

Karen M.R. Townsend, Ph.D.
KTownsend Consulting

"*Leadership Soul* is a practical, educational, and inspirational guide to help you continue to develop your leadership skills. I challenge you to open any chapter and not find something that you could immediately use in your day to day interactions with your team. So grab a highlighter, because you will find yourself referring back to this book often. If you want to leverage higher competence to create higher levels of productivity and profitability, then I recommend you buy Kendall C. Wright's book."

Patrick Donadio, MBA, CSP™, MCC
Communication Strategist, Executive Coach & Author of
Communicating with Impact

I have worked in the space of Leadership and Culture for the past 18 years. I have read a copious number of books attended seminars, conferences, and many mastermind groups globally. In each era there will come a book which will change things, Leadership Soul is such a book whether you are starting, or a seasoned Leader make this book your constant companion and observe the change in yourself and your organization. I would urge you to give this book to as many Leaders as a gift so that this revolutionary work becomes the new Agenda for Leaders. Kendall C. Wright has cracked the Leadership code with this book…

Billy Selekane CSP, SASHoF, EXPY - Africa's Highest
Designated Professional Speaker
Executive Chairman
Intelligent Edge Consulting

"Kendall Wright is a genius at engaging his audience… Intelligent. Innovative. Authentic. Provocative. Leadership Soul is genuinely him. It's an absolutely necessary epistle for the modern leader… Signed, Sealed, and Delivered!"

Tim Coleman

The teaching of great leadership is something I feel is rapidly becoming a lost art. Just when I was ready to give up finding great literature that captures formal expectations and needed tools for today's leaders; Enter *Leadership Soul*!

Kendall has infused the greatest musical era of our time, with an in-depth journey of tools for great leadership. I remember reading the list of chapters. The first thing I wanted to do was call Kendall to ask him a simple question. "Sir, where was this book 23 years ago?" I could have used these most important teachings when I started my career with the YMCA of Greater Cincinnati.

"I CAN'T HELP MYSELF," would have been the go-to chapter that would have offered me enhanced clarity in my newfound role.

Ten years later, after accepting the position, as the Middletown YMCA, Executive Director. UPSIDE DOWN (INSIDE OUT) would have given me a broader view of the measure of change I was encountering.

Presently working for the United Way of Greater Cincinnati, as the Middletown Area Executive Director, Leadership Soul will be my guiding light for the rest of my professional journey. I truly endorse this book as a necessary read for all present-day and future leaders.

Kendall, congratulation to a dear friend and excellent role model!

Terrence Sherrer Sr.
Middletown *Area Executive Director*
United Way of Greater Cincinnati

"I have known Kendall many years and have always appreciated his knowledge and insights into leadership development. Leadership Soul is a perfect example of Kendall's grasp of the human condition and how it can be optimized in any leadership setting. I highly recommend taking time to absorb his wisdom. Don't be surprised if you catch yourself tapping your foot, as you recall the music of these great Motown songs! Kudos to Kendall Wright!!"

Earl R. Major
Vice President, Human Resources
Delta Dental *of Michigan, Ohio, and Indiana*

It is with pleasure I provide my endorsement for this brilliant work. I have always had a great deal of respect for Kendall's depth of knowledge and experience in Leadership Development, Motivational Speaking, Facilitation, and Training. This presentation is a gift that is sure to bless many. Just paging through the table of contents will engage the layman and music lover alike. I applaud Kendall and his team for this brilliant idea and for the care and erudition that went into this body of work. Bravo!

Grant Doster
SVP Global *Inclusive Leadership, LHH*

Kendall's creative, thought-provoking, and insightful coup with *Leadership Soul* is perfectly timed, as leaders at all levels today face challenges that even the financial crashes of recent decades could not surpass.

Kendall and I first came together to collaborate on a global client's intervention focusing on leadership and inclusion. I was very grateful to have felt his generosity and also witnessed, listened, and absorbed his philosophies on the critical role of leadership as he questioned, provoked, and inspired some of the best leaders with his "tough-love" approach.

It is an absolute necessity for leaders to build trust and connection in todays' new ways of working, which Kendall describes with brilliant clarity on how to deal with specific leadership challenges in each chapter. I have also downloaded these 21 Motown classics as a favorite playlist, which as I listen to over again, have become strong metaphors for guiding leaders through the maze of complexity the world faces today.

Kingsley Weber
Founding Partner, CEO Solutions Ltd

I have found that leadership requires our heads to be skyward, but also know there will be some wins and some losses!

I'm sure that these 21Soulful Leadership Lessons; will show you the will and the way to demonstrate the kind of leadership that God our Father desires and will make you strive for and believe that the SKY is the limit!

Rev. Gregory Tyus
Senior Pastor, *United Missionary Baptist Church*

Kendall has been a business owner and a leader within organizations for decades, and the reader reaps the benefit of his experiences and wisdom in *Leadership Soul: 21 Soulful Leadership Lessons from Motown Hits*. His own style—charismatic and engaging, with a strong bent toward results—is reflected in his words.

Kendall shares the leadership skills and mindsets that underpin the track records of successful leaders and identifies the behaviors that any leader can use to capture the hearts and minds of associates. Engaged associates create strong and successful businesses.

Leadership Soul captures a variety of current leadership challenges and provides the reader with tested and practical approaches that are useful and smart. The author delights in his content as he skillfully weaves in backstories and nuggets on beloved Motown groups and sounds, as well as information and anecdotes from businesses the reader will recognize. Each leader challenge includes strategies that guide the reader toward effective outcomes and wraps up with a succinct Soulful Leadership Lesson.

Well-crafted and delightful to read, *Leadership Soul* will make you hum the Motown hits while you're reading, and maybe pick up an earworm or two! The lessons are so valuable, however, that you'll find yourself revisiting them and leaving with new and actionable bits of wisdom every time.

Janine Moon
Certified Executive Coach / Master Certified Career Coach
Workforce Change
Author: Career Ownership: Creating ‹Job Security› in Any
Economy
Career Partnering: A New Model for Today›s Talent

DEDICATION

I dedicate this work to all who invested in me when all I had to offer in return was sweat equity. Thank you for sharing your faith, trust, and wisdom. May the ripples of your influence and insights continue to wash up upon shorelines that never saw your footprint.

CONTENTS

ACKNOWLEDGMENTS

I must first praise and thank my God, the Almighty. Without His grace and mercy, none of this would have been possible. I want to thank the legion of workshop participants, clients, audience members, and unsuspecting airline seatmates who allowed me to test and refine the philosophies and practices presented in this work. To all those loyal and persistent fans who continually asked, "When are you going to write that book?" I say thank you for your motivating influences.

I want to thank Kevin Aldridge and J. Phillip Holloman for the extraordinary assistance they provided in getting this project into your hands.

Thank you to my wife, Marva, and to my children for inspiring and encouraging me, particularly through the very rough times. Your expectations of me are nourishment and fuel to my soul.

To all who helped in any way, I say thank you.

FOREWORD

I wish I had this book, Leadership Soul, 40 years ago, at the start of my professional career. I would have read it initially, reread it at each promotion or change in assignment, and referred to it often during my career journey.

My career journey ultimately led to me becoming the President & COO of the Cintas Corporation. My leadership style and behavior evolved over time based on my core values and through observing other leaders, both good and bad. I internalized the traits of good leaders and learned what not to emulate from bad leaders. Having the 21 essential lessons from Leadership Soul would have made me a better leader faster.

Kendall and I grew up in Middletown, Ohio. We lived in the same community and attended the same public schools and were members of the same church, United Missionary Baptist Church. United was born out of the merger of three Baptist churches; the church was also the epicenter of the Civil Rights Movement in Middletown during the 1960s and early 1970s. The three-church merger and the Civil Rights Movement required great soulful leadership. Through observation and participation, our aspiring leadership journeys began.

Kendall went on to become an accomplished and internationally acclaimed leadership coach, consultant, workshop facilitator, author, and keynote speaker. On a global scale, he has helped countless leaders/managers/students from an assorted range of industries and sectors in understanding and leveraging the human dynamics of leadership.

The Motown Hook! Kendall uses Motown hits as the theme for each of his 21 essential leadership lessons. I grew up listening to the Motown sound. When a new hit came out, and you heard the song on the radio or at a party, it was the music and the beat that initially caused your engagement. When you purchased the album or "45" (old school vinyl), and you played the tunes over and over, the lyrics reached your heart, mind, and soul. The great Motown artists told stories, provided life lessons, explained relationship dynamics, and even raised your social consciousness. It's the lyrics that still resonate with me today, 50 years later.

I draw a clear distinction between leadership and management. You lead people–You manage processes. Leadership Soul is about effective, authentic leadership; the leader's mindset, prerequisite traits, skill set, behavior, and understanding the human dynamic. For each of the essential leadership lessons, Kendall brings to life organizational/team situations that are mishandled (or not handled) by leaders resulting in unintended consequences and poor results. He then provides the key learnings, the required mindset, strategies, and guidelines for becoming an accomplished leader.

Leadership Soul will expand your leadership comprehension quotient if you internalize the 21 essential lessons and let the lessons permeate your leadership authentic self. Leadership Soul will make you a much better leader faster.

J. Phillip Holloman
Former President/COO, Cintas Corporation

PREFACE

Many might question the need for another leadership book, but practically everywhere you turn, you'll find evidence of leadership deficiencies, ineptitude, arrogance, and other destructive shortcomings. Surveys and polls substantiate that there are two root causes of the serious problems plaguing the leadership ranks: a.) a high level of ignorance regarding the topic; and b.) gross skill outages. As such, this state of affairs evidences the need for leaders to be better (differently) informed and equipped to meet the demands of leading in today's hyperactive, hyper-connected, and hyper-dynamic global marketplace.

I have spent practically the entirety of my career serving as a leader and educating leaders. Over the decades, it became painfully obvious that there was a need for another voice, a distinctive voice, in the leadership dialogue. Given the new structures, paradigms, and models for conducting global business – and their resulting human dynamics, I believe I am distinctively positioned to be that voice. As the adage says, "If you find a need, fill it."

Let me be the first to concede that "leadership truth" may be universal, but its presentation is often unique to its messenger.

Many times, how something is said, can be equally or even more important than what was said. With that point in mind, I don't have a secret formula to unveil or magic pixie dust with which to douse you, but I do have sound and tested philosophy, principles, and practices forged from my wide-ranging experiences and insights that I present in my tested, proven, even venerated style. You are going to love what is awaiting you on every page. I'm anticipating that these tools, techniques, and tips will strongly resonant with you. Even more importantly, they will prove themselves efficacious.

The *Leadership Soul* project is unique - and it is special. This project is both innovative by way of its thematic premise and engaging by way of its conceptual platform. By evoking the power of timeless Motown tunes, and pairing those tunes to many of the most frustrating challenges of leadership, I have created an executive leadership course whose soundtrack is integral to the curriculum. That soulful soundtrack makes for a phenomenally lively musical backdrop. The musical references provide the emotional anchor to ensure these exceptional leadership lessons are adhesive and readily applicable.

It is time to put on some comfortable shoes! There is no doubt that as you progress through this paradigm-shifting experience, you are going to dance, move, and shout. In the words of the greatest ambassador of soulful rhythms, the late Mr. Don Cornelius, "You Can Bet Your Last Money; It's Gonna Be A Stone Gas, Honey!"

INTRODUCTION

"Leadership!!!"

At least that's how it seems most people think of the topic. For them, the idea of leadership is enveloped in ever-escalating enthusiasm and excitement. In reality, the more common experience is not "Leadership!!!" but instead, "Leadership???"

Is there a concept any more elusive than leadership? Even more elusive than the concept is the quest to meet or exceed its many nebulous and often arbitrary tenets. If you are among the millions of individuals saddled with leadership responsibilities but struggling to find your groove, this pioneering resource is just for you.

If you are tired of feeling flustered as team and performance situations continue to devolve, this resource is exactly the remedy you need. If you are committed to expanding your awareness, enhancing your skill set, and delivering outstanding personal and team results, you have found the perfect resource to assist you in achieving your leadership goals.

The material contained in the pages of this book is crafted and curated to specifically address the shared concerns of countless leaders who struggle to address issues of authenticity, appreciation, accountability, as well as onboarding, team building, and conflict resolution. This project is like finding a streaming service that intuitively plays the very song you need to hear - exactly when you need to hear it.

In this project, your favorite Motown tunes are utilized in an allegorical framework to present priceless insights and powerful tools aimed toward expanding and enhancing your leadership effectiveness.

Baby, I'm For Real

7 Guidelines for Unveiling Your Authenticity

"Leaders who create questions about their authenticity in small things will be deemed untrustworthy in grand things."

Alexander Nix, CEO of Cambridge Analytica, was immediately suspended by the Board of Directors. This action was the result of Nix's inauthentic representation of data acquisition and use by Facebook during the 2016 presidential election. The Board's official statement read, "In the view of the board, Mr. Nix's recent comments secretly recorded by Channel 4 and other allegations do not represent the values or operations of the firm, and his suspension reflects the seriousness with which we view this violation."

In their hearts, they knew they were the real deal. However, the spotlight never shone brightly on The Originals until they were allowed to display their unique synergies. The Originals weren't thought of by most as anything more than a background group, but they were fortunate to have in their professional network a couple of very influential people who pushed them to find "their" sound. When that happened, the extraordinarily talented quartet found themselves celebrating a number one hit. Their million-selling, chart-topper, "Baby, I'm For Real," erupted in 1969, and remains a well-loved classic to this day.

What was the key to The Originals' success? The answer to that question isn't limited solely to advancing the success of a singing group, but it also has great and grand application to your success as a leader. The profundity surrounding their success is overwhelming. Follow this: the first number one hit for a group called The Originals was the result of them doing something different from what they, and others, had been doing for so long. In reality, The Originals' success was the result of a two-step process. First, searching themselves, and second, stretching themselves. Their success was the result of tapping into their authentic selves and expressing their talent as only they could. Moreover, if that's not weighty enough, consider this: their vehicle of expression just happened to be a song entitled, "Baby, I'm For Real."

If you were to "grab the mic" at the start of your next team meeting and profess, "Baby, I'm for real!" as a proclamation of your authenticity, how would your team members and peers react? After getting over the shock of it all, would your team members and peers agree with your assertion or would they politely remain mum in passive disagreement?

While the colloquialism "Baby, I'm for real" may not be appropriate in most work environments, there is no denying that the implied pledge and promise would be welcomed and readily embraced. *In fact, employees, peers, and associates long for something that is desperately missing in their work environments. That missing element is authenticity, and more specifically, authenticity on behalf of their leaders. Employees long for interactions and information that isn't shaded, shrouded, or spun.* However, for most employees, that is a longing that continues to go unfulfilled.

Why is it that so few employees really know their leaders? It might be because the leaders are too busy concealing and disguising their true selves in an attempt to become what they believe they should be or have to be. Perhaps these leaders are allergic to authenticity and either deliberately, or otherwise, avoid presenting their authentic selves. The bottom line is that it becomes increasingly more difficult to trust a leader who seems to be intentionally evasive or elusive. This is true and isn't up for debate; inauthentic leadership carries with it many detractions. *One of the major consequences of inauthentic leadership is an incredulous and irresolute workforce.*

Some of the "old school" thinkers will zealously retort, "You have to keep a distance between yourself and those in your direct report." There is no doubt that these old-school pundits are thoroughly convinced, aggressively vocal, and their mantra is utterly pervasive. In fact, I am sure you've heard it and can recite it flawlessly. The mantra is, "Familiarity breeds contempt." Regardless of their conviction and the pervasiveness of that ideology, I respectfully note that those old-school minds are misguided. That old-school mindset contributes to a phenomenon I labeled - Exaggerated Anonymity. If there were ever an era in which the fundamental assumptions embedded in that old manta needed to be reevaluated, if not strongly challenged, clearly it is the current era in which we lead.

It is never wise to disclose, indiscriminately, personal information to strangers or employees. That is not the way to build healthy and respectful relationships, nor is it what authenticity in leadership requires. Discretion is still an invaluable asset. However, because you are leading people, you should remember people need connection. **If your employees don't feel they have connected with the real you, meaning the authentic you, the chances are high that their trust levels will be low. As a principle, each leader should come to terms with the fact that there is an inverse correlation between leadership authenticity and employee disengagement. The more inauthentic the leader is in his or her interactions, the lower the levels of employee engagement. Conversely, employee disengagement declines as the level of authenticity increases.**

Straightforwardly, authenticity is the state or condition of being free of obfuscation. You might think of authenticity as being genuine, reliable, and trustworthy. This is what so many employees are missing in their relationships with their leaders. The employees experience the leaders as distant, dispassionate, and duplicitous. Subsequently, employees reciprocate what is given to them. So, the employees become equally as distant, dispassionate, and duplicitous. As a way to safeguard against these predictable byproducts of exaggerated anonymity, leaders must be intentional in their efforts to "humanize" themselves. Leaders must be intentional in presenting and honoring both their plans to advance the teams' productivity and their promises of transparency of conduct and approach.

More and more evidence is published each day, some anecdotal and some empirical, all very revealing as to the power of authenticity in leadership. In a recent study conducted by the University of Las Vegas, researchers discovered that leaders, who were rated as being more authentic by just 1 point on a 5-point scale, precipitated a 26% improvement in their employees' level of commitment to the organization. Call it engagement, call it inclusion, or call it retention. No matter what you call it, it all means increased productivity and profitability. These bottom-line measures of success directly reflect the effectiveness of leadership.

Is it just a coincidence that the words author and authenticity share the same beginning four letters? I suggest to you that we, as leaders, are in fact, authors. We are writing new chapters of our leadership narrative with each interaction we have with those in our sphere of influence. In fact, we are writing with indelible ink. As leaders, we write on the hearts and minds of our employees with each comment, interaction, or encounter. Your conduct is your implement, and their hearts, minds, and souls are the scrolls.

The importance and impact of authenticity in leadership are questioned by many and misunderstood by even more. However, this is to be expected of any severely countercultural approach to leadership. If it challenges the prevailing method of the day, expect resistance. To that point, it appears that the German philosopher, Arthur Schopenhauer, was correct when he quipped, "All truth passes through three stages. First, it is ridiculed. Second, it is violently opposed. Third, it is accepted as being self-evident."

Now would be an excellent time for you – leader - to begin singing, "Baby, I'm For Real." Again, there is no question as to whether or not your employees need affirmation of your authenticity – they do. The affirmation of your authenticity, specifically via congruence of word and deed, is desperately needed given employee trust levels are generally low and appear headed lower. To reiterate a point made earlier, it is difficult to increase trust between you - the leader - and your employees, if the employees feel their leader is an enigma. *If they don't know you, or at least feel as if they do, then you best prepare for stern resistance, second-guessing, and their frequent imputation of negative motives to your actions.* I think it is fair to say that authenticity is an effective antidote to many of the counterproductive behaviors in most organizations today.

It only makes sense that the challenges of society would find a toehold in your organization. That means what is happening in the "outside world" will also manifest in the "inside world" of your organization. Recently, an AP-Gfk poll, a collaboration between the Associated Press and one of the largest international market research organizations, found that Americans are principally suspicious, even in routine everyday interactions. The poll revealed that 66% of Americans believe "others" can't generally be trusted. A leader who routinely opts for or defaults to inauthentic interactions with employees, peers, and key stakeholders fuels these perceptions of suspicion.

What are the consequences of hiding behind a veil of inauthenticity? What you already know, even intuitively, is that this type of leadership comes with a price, a very high price. According to research reported by Stephen M. R. Covey, only 49% of the employee base trusts senior management. That means that more than half of all employees distrust the individuals charting the course for their organizations. Stunning!

You can't spin this data enough to make this state of affairs sound healthy or promising. Covey went on to highlight that 72% of employees don't consider the CEO to be a credible source of information. Sadly, if you can't trust the chief executive, who can you trust? I would add the question: how authentic are those CEOs in the perception of their employees? Let's face it, in the absence of authenticity, very few good outcomes are obtained or sustained long-term.

You may not be a CEO, but in principle, when it comes to building trust, your challenge is no less daunting. To gain the trust and respect of your employees, you must allow a more authentic expression of who you are to permeate each interaction. Your team members have to know you; they have to believe that you have their best interests at heart and will fight for them. Your employees have to be convinced that you are the real deal, not some charlatan only looking to use them as stepping-stones to a corner office, special assignment, or stewardship role.

Leaders, in what are now ever-increasing numbers, are realizing that authenticity is the new leadership currency. Don't come to the workplace without it, or you will find the marketplace closed for business.

If you are looking to produce out-of-the-box results, you will have to come out of the box of pretense, superiority, and fear. In the words of Socrates, "The way to gain a good reputation is to endeavor to be what you desire to appear."

Being a more authentic leader doesn't mean you have "no filters" or that you don't use good judgment. In leadership, to lack either is to directly and deliberately jeopardize your effectiveness, as well as your future. Instead, authenticity in leadership encompasses a coalescence of courage, caring, and competence. This means you as the leader must possess the courage to challenge the status quo, care enough about the people to keep them well informed, and command the competence to use the appropriate degree of discretion befitting each situation.

Authentic leaders are different from other leaders in a number of key ways. If you desire to differentiate yourself from the also-rans by producing culture-impacting, market-shaping results, become a student of the great ones and learn why they do what they do. Here are 7 guidelines for becoming a more authentic leader in today's frenetic and erratic workplace.

Get Confident in Your Identity. Knowing who you are, who you really are, is key to finding the courage to resist the temptation to question your judgment, your value, or your effectiveness. A strong self-identity empowers you to take a confident stand for what is just and what is right.

Firm Up Your Philosophy on Failure. How you perceive failure will dictate how you present yourself to your team and peers. If you don't understand that failure is an incident, not an identity, you will be singularly preoccupied with hiding your flaws and denying your shortcomings. Come to terms with failure as a part of the developmental process and free yourself to be your authentic self.

Make Known Your Intention. Call it the power of suggestion or just guided perception, but it helps to let your team know that you are working to become an even more authentic leader. The benefits include the introduction of the topic for team discussion, and perhaps, an increased likelihood of receiving specific feedback that you weren't privy to prior. Another great benefit is that your declaration transforms your team into a community of accountability partners.

Use the E.L.M. As Your Guidon. Having your vision fixed on, and decisions informed by, an incontrovertible guidon is an awesome source of power and comfort. That power and comfort come from faithfully measuring potential actions against a standard that is Ethical, Legal, and Moral. Authentic leaders are relentlessly committed to principle over popularity. Authentic leaders consistently and predictably choose that which is principled over what is popular.

Admit Your Mistakes, Master the Lesson. Your team members will be inspired by your successes, but they will be instructed by your mistakes. In fact, your mistakes are the core curriculum of your mentorship. As unnatural and unbelievable as it may seem, sharing your mistakes - and the lessons learned - serves to humanize you and increases your authenticity as a leader.

Make Follow Up & Follow Through Your Trademark. People are evaluating your long-term fidelity on just a few basic criteria: do you follow up and do you follow through. In the minds of your employees, congruence of word and deed is integral to authenticity. For them, incongruence and a cavalier attitude regarding that incongruence is a clear signpost of inauthenticity. If you want others to regard you as an authentic leader, simply do what you say you are going to do.

Perceptive of EQ, IQ, and PQ. The ability to monitor and interpret the interplay of Emotional Intelligence (feel), Intelligence Quotient (know), and Proficiency Quotient (do) is a key asset of an Authentic Leader. Attentiveness to your balance of these three variables and the presence or absence of that balance in others empowers you to create the right connection and a positive impact.

These 7 guidelines will help you present the most authentic "you" to your team members, peers, and key stakeholders. Mastery of this list represents an investment in your professional and personal development that is truly worth any of the associated inconveniences. Remember, your goal is to grab the mic and sing with all your heart "Baby, I'm For Real" - without any fear of contradiction or challenge.

Soulful Leadership Lesson: Authenticity is the new leadership currency. Given this fact, your authenticity is dramatically devalued if you subscribe to the limiting mindset and methodologies of exaggerated anonymity. As leaders grow strong in their self-identities, they are less fearful of being open, honest, and vulnerable. Authentic leaders are unremittingly committed to principle over popularity. They consistently and predictably choose that which is principled over what is popular.

The Boss

7 Cognitive Variances of The Boss Vs. Leader Archetype

"If you don't have the skills to be an Actualizing Leader, you will default to being a boss; and in most cases, a really bad boss."

An employee at Day and Night Spa in Mount Prospect, IL, told police that her boss Alex "Daddy" Campbell forced her to get three tattoos. One was a horseshoe - a "brand" he made all his female employees get - and another, on the back of her neck, was the number "917" representing Campbell's birthday. All the female workers at the "massage parlor" were illegal immigrants from Belarus and Ukraine. The boss made it a practice to confiscate their passports and visas, thus making them his prisoners. To ensure their compliance, Campbell taped the women having sex with him and with each other.

Campbell's first trial was dismissed after it was discovered that his defense attorney was a "client" at the parlor. Campbell was ultimately convicted on 11 counts and faces life in prison.

Back in May of 1979 when Diana Ross topped the charts with her disco-inspired hit *The Boss*, our nation and our world were dramatically different from what we see and hear today.

Back then, no one conceived of congressional debates over a $15 minimum wage. No one thought that television programs such as *Modern Family, The Big Bang, and The Walking Dead* could be so popular and wildly profitable. No one really believed that the ace of a Little League World Series could be – a girl. No one envisioned that a German automobile manufacturer, whose reputation was built on innovative engineering, would face the largest fine in history, potentially $18 billion, for EPA violations in the United States.

Yes, things are a bit different today than they were in 1979. Not only is disco not a thing anymore (does anyone even remember how to do the Hustle?), but certain words or terms today have taken on a blustering life of their own. For example, consider the term "boss."

So, is it just me, or have you also noticed the pervasive (and annoying) use of the term boss?

Today, there is a rather distracting, if not disturbing, trend in both popular and organizational culture centering on the use of the term boss. Dare I say the trend isn't just over usage of the term, but more so a troubling escalating glamorization of the term. Of late, "to be a boss," to do something "like a boss," or to be addressed as a "boss" has gained wide-ranging appeal and acceptance in a variety of circles and settings.

In 1979, if you heard the term boss, particularly in major media, it routinely referenced people such as Carlo "Don Carlo" Gambino,

Anthony "Fat Tony" Salerno, and Paul "Big Paulie" Castellano. In other words, boss was shorthand for Mob Boss. However, that isn't the case so much today.

My disconcerting encounters with the term seem endless and unavoidable. Recently, I participated in a webinar during which the presenters addressed the participants as "bosses." As if that wasn't enough, in the social media space, I saw the hashtag #LikeABoss. Is there no escape? My day continued to spiral downward when I saw a commercial introducing a new behemoth of a bacon cheeseburger called - you guessed it -- The Bacon Boss.

The proliferation in the use of the term boss is readily evident in the workplace as well. It isn't unusual to hear someone refer to the boss's office, or having to go see the boss. And let's not forget the classic adage, "What the boss wants, the boss gets." The term echoes in hallways, conference rooms, and break rooms across the country. Amazingly, even a cursory search on Amazon turns up nearly 16,000 book titles containing the word boss. Clearly, the term is well accounted for in the everyday jargon and lexicon of most organizations.

And while it is true that the most popular and contemporary understanding of the term pertains to the arena of work, it is also true that now may be the perfect time to rethink the use of the term in today's more collaborative and respectful workplaces. Just as time hasn't been extremely kind to disco, it may also be time to bid the term boss an impassive and solemn fare thee well.

My informal interviews with individuals from various walks of life, geographies, generations, and genders regarding how they perceive the term boss in relation to the term leader, verified that for the majority of people the two terms are near, if not exact, synonyms. However, we shouldn't make the mistake of assuming that just because words are identified as synonyms that those words impart identical *emotional* impact.

Words are vessels that contain and convey import, power, and passions. It would be foolish to attempt to discount or dismiss the fact that certain words have historical "baggage" and emotional impact not shared by their synonyms. And even though the contemporary connotation of a term may change, certain vessels retain a caustic and noxious residue. For those select terms, their impact is often more easily sensed than articulated, but that impact is present nonetheless. Such is the case with the term boss.

Generally, people may not ascribe a significant difference between the terms leader and boss. And in fact, they may freely use the terms interchangeably. However, when asked to explore the emotional components of the terms a clear distinction emerges. Don't make the mistake of thinking this emotional aspect is inconsequential. It is not. In fact, this emotional distinction may be a true gateway to understanding the crucial, but elusive, differentiation between the terms leader and boss. Perhaps even more importantly, by understanding the reasons for this difference in emotional charge, we can preempt many unintended consequences.

This nearly instinctual and virtually visceral reaction to the term boss isn't merely coincidental. There is some overtly reprehensible history associated with the word. The term finds its origins in the Dutch language. A quick review of its etymology and usage reveals a menacing legacy of intimidation, mayhem, and even murder. Denotatively, boss is said to be the Americanization of the mid-17th-century Dutch term - *baas*. Originally, baas referred to one's owner, master, or foreman. Connotatively, *"The baas"* was one having the authority to <u>beat an underling into submission and compliance</u>.

The term boss takes on a decidedly racial element when inspected through the lens of its South African history and usage. In South Africa, "baas" was the term used to refer to a white person in a position of authority over "blacks and coloureds." In light of that history, for many in the workforce, around the globe, the term boss carries categorically negative karma.

Over the past several decades, we have seen a shift toward utilizing language and phrases that promote respect, inclusion, and peerness. Such examples include replacing the term handicap with the phrase person with a disability or differently abled. Other examples include addressing adult females as women instead of girls. Shifting from the use of Hispanic to Latino and the use of sexual orientation instead of sexual preference. Each shift was geared toward enhancing the quality of the relationship and promoting a more respectful work environment. Therefore, with the goal of respect and the enhancement of relationships in mind, the term boss must be retired from our conversation, and especially from our workplace conversations.

Given that we don't normally address those we value and respect using terms or titles that communicate the contrary, then the term boss should be understood as a derogatory and disrespectful term, and duly eschewed.

Very few (if any) job descriptions actually use the title boss. In our everyday conversations, we must replace the term boss with the actual title of the role, or some abbreviation of that title. Either way, it would be a far cry better than to continue to refer to supervisors, team leads, managers, etc., as bosses or big bosses.

A word of caution to those captivated by the idea of being called boss, as well to those who feel compelled to address others by that term - you may be unwittingly setting yourself up for unwelcomed, unhealthy, and unproductive interpersonal dynamics.

It is very important to note here, that with any new awareness also comes a new level of accountability. Language is powerful. It can be a powerful tool or a powerful weapon.

Your relationships are either healed or harmed by language. This is true whether the relationship occurs inside or outside the workplace. Normally, words with bad karma - words with origins mired in an extensive history of dehumanization, denigration, disrespect, and death - don't contribute positively to healthy, progressive, and productive relationships.

I submit to you that the "boss mentality," whether embraced by a supervisor or conceded and consented to by an employee, is at the root of much of the dysfunction your team is experiencing. Don't be fooled; this boss mentality is pervasive and pernicious. The boss mentality is evidenced or characterized by intimidation, fear of making mistakes, acquiescence, and low engagement. In a well-choreographed dance of collusion, both supervisor and employee create an environment that systematically eviscerates all hope of trust, initiative, authentic collaboration, and innovation. Predictably, the boss mentality results in an oppressive and repressive culture.

It seems highly unlikely that anything remotely resembling optimal performance can be achieved as long as the boss mentality is allowed to reign and rule within your organizational culture.

The odds are that you have seen one or more of the seemingly ubiquitous charts, memes, and illustrations contrasting the traits and tendencies of a boss to those of a leader. With ridiculous and even annoying regularity, one such chart shows up in my LinkedIn updates or Facebook newsfeed. Interestingly, these representations routinely fail to identify the cause of the grossly divergent patterns of conduct they depict. Instead, the diagrams merely present the symptoms as evidence of the differences, but not the actual cause.

The real contrast between a leader and a boss begins in the mind. There lies the cause of the grossly divergent patterns of conduct between a leader and a boss. To paraphrase a wise prophet, as a man thinketh, so is he.

The mind is the seedbed of the boss mentally. Literally, it begins with how the individual "in charge" regards and references those in his or her direct report. I refer to this as "cognitive suiting." How the "supervisor" perceives those in his or her direct report will dictate the leadership approach adopted and practices pursued. Ultimately, the process of cognitive suiting dictates how the "supervisor" opts to interact with employees. Cognitive suiting sets the tone and tenor of all subsequent interactions.

If we could get inside the head of the boss and contrast what we find there to what is in the mind of the leader, we would find 7 key areas of the variance in how each regards those under their charge:

- **Rank**   **Relative position within a hierarchy**
- **Role**   **The function in which the employee works**
- **Value**   **Relative importance, direct impact, to the success of the enterprise**
- **Capacity**   **Facility to analyze, synthesize, and extrapolate information**
- **Mobility**   **Interest and ability to make vertical and lateral moves**
- **Motivation**   **The driving force behind an employee's decisions**
- **Humanity**   **Respecting the "wholeness" of the employee**

Following are details as to how the boss and the leader differ in their perspectives of direct reports in these 7 key areas:

Rank: Bosses tend to default to an assumption of their innate superiority, assuming everyone is inferior (in practically every way) to him or herself. Leaders, while being aware of where an individual's position may fall in the hierarchy, don't allow rank to influence how they regard the individual or to shadow how the leader assesses the individual's contributions.

Role: Bosses tend to pigeonhole and discount individuals based on the type of work that an individual does in the organization. Conversely, leaders are preoccupied with what the individual has to offer independent of what the individual's role happens to be in the organization.

Value: Bosses assess an employee's value based on how directly and significantly the employee contributes to the bottom line. Bosses value rainmakers while devaluing support staff. Leaders see and understand that the contributions of each team member are integral to the overall success of the organization.

Capacity: Bosses tend to underestimate and undervalue the employee's potential for growth and development. Leaders look to leverage an employee's potential to its fullest.

Mobility: Bosses tend to think an employee isn't able or interested in moving up or around in the organization. Leaders encourage employees to continue to grow, explore, and expand.

Motivation: Bosses believe employees are always looking to "get over" by looking to do as little as possible. Bosses often complain of employees being lazy and feeling entitled. Leaders believe employees earnestly desire to make a fair and substantive contribution toward the advancement of the business.

Humanity: Bosses tend to think of employees as interchangeable cogs in an automated system. For the boss, there isn't much difference in their perception of inventory and headcount. Bosses view people as an unfortunate but necessary annoyance. Leaders respect and honor the employee as a whole person not just a set of hands, a strong back, or a leased brain. Leaders embrace the uniqueness of the team members and promote respect of that individuality.

There you have them; the 7 ways bosses and leaders cognitively suit their direct reports. These stark contrasts in perspectives result in stark contrasts in leadership philosophies and practices. Leaders, particularly those who are most well suited for the demands of the multicultural work environment, tend to anchor their perceptions on the positive end of each continuum, while bosses tend to hunker down on the negative end.

The transformation from boss to leader is not as simple as changing a name badge. It requires some very deep and focused introspection and the subsequent redefining of the leadership relationship. Anything short of that is sure to evaporate in the heat of adversity and a tough economic environment.

To aid you in the transition from boss to leader, here are 8 imperatives:

- **Lose the intimidation routine**
- **Make respect a priority in <u>every</u> interaction**
- **Aggressively counter your negative assumptions about your direct reports**
- **Learn to (really) listen**
- **See people for "who" they are, not merely for "what" they do**
- **Ask questions; don't assume you have all the answers**
- **Start taking responsibility; stop blaming, and start sharing the credit**
- **Become intimately acquainted with humility and forgo haughtiness**

Your style of leadership can propel a team forward or leave both team members and productivity petrified. Over time, bosses essentially douse the fires of innovation, collaboration, and initiative. Of course, that is exactly the opposite of what is required to grow an enterprise. To get your team and your organization on the track to higher productivity, profitability, and respect, you must get rid of all vestiges of the boss mentality. The result of your efforts will be more than obvious as you watch your team grow healthier and more productive day by day.

Diana Ross could be "the Boss" on the disco floor, but having bosses on the shop floor, in the conference room, or in the lab is sure to be demotivating, disheartening, and lead to higher levels of dysfunction within your organization. Replace bossing with leading!

Soulful Leadership Lesson: The term boss has a nefarious history and is far from a term of respect or endearment. Given that we don't normally address those we value and respect by terms or titles that communicate the contrary, then the term boss should be duly eschewed. Leaders and bosses see their direct reports differently, actually in conflicting and contrasting ways. This cognitive divergence results in marked behavioral differences between a boss and a leader. Bosses tend to view their employees as little more than a means to an end, while leaders tend to respect and value the "whole" person while pursuing the highest quality of the work relationships possible.

Just My Imagination (Running Away With Me)

The Cost And Consequence Of Imaginary Competence

"The harder your team has to look to find your leadership skills, the harder you'll have to look to find team members."

Is there a more ubiquitous entity in the land of tech than Google? In its early years, Google was a struggling startup like so many other thousands of startups. At that point, the leaders of Excite, today know as Ask.com, had the opportunity to acquire Google for a pittance - $750,000. Yet, those leaders concluded not only was the price too high but that the future wasn't very bright for Google. So, Excite passed on the opportunity. Well, I am sure you know how that decision turned out. Today, Google is worth approximately $365 billion.

"Now, imagine this…"

We know from experience that when a sentence starts with those words, it is an explicit invitation to utilize one of the most powerful tools known to humankind – the imagination.

The human imagination is amazing and can be put to use for either noble or nefarious causes. The imagination has the power to hypothesize the architecture of an atomic bomb, conceptualize the creation of the Life Straw, or devise the protocols for robotic-assisted heart surgery. Great thinkers, "Imagineers" as they are sometimes called, such as Leonardo da Vinci, Dr. Patricia Bath, George Washington Carver, and Granville T. Woods, and so many others were the inquisitive protégées of powerful and active imaginations. We owe much to the amazing imagination.

And while the imagination plays an influential role in the innovation of wonderful technological advances and medical breakthroughs, it also plays an indispensable role in matters of the heart. In fact, there is a song that aptly illustrates this point. In 1971, The Temptations returned to the top of the music charts with "Just My Imagination." This classic song puts the power of the imagination on full display as a young man fantasizes about a loving, happy, and exciting life with a young woman with whom he is completely infatuated. The problem is – the young lady doesn't even know he exists.

The stories of imaginations working overtime in the real world are very familiar, and as familiar as they are, their consequences are nonetheless unnerving. Who could forget the story of the love-stricken U.S. teenager who flew 7,000 miles from Ohio to the Zhejiang province of China? The teen embarked on his epic excursion because he thought he had made a love connection over the internet. In his mind, he found his true love, his princess, and was ready to begin a fairytale romance in which he and his sweetheart lived happily ever after.

Perhaps not so surprisingly, the young man was sternly rebuffed, thoroughly dejected, and in short order, completely broke. Chinese police eventually found the would-be suitor unconscious, inebriated, and suffering from hypothermia along the bank of the Xu River. How could this happen? How could he be so wrong? Surely, there can be no question as to whether or not this young man's imagination had indeed gotten the best of him.

The challenge of the unbridled imagination, an imagination that overrules reality, is not foreign to the workplace, especially among the ranks of leadership. In fact, some employees and researchers claim that the problem of leaders misusing their imaginations, thinking more highly of themselves than they ought, is so commonplace that it is treated as a given. Well, a given maybe, but welcomed - not at all. ***I contend that the imagination is easily the most often abused and misused tool of leadership.***

The resulting challenges of the misused imagination are many, but the specific challenge addressed here isn't related to leaders conceiving elaborate strategies and schemes too grand for implementation. Instead, the specific challenge confronted here is the repeated overestimation of leadership competence.

Several years ago, two researchers from Cornell University, Justin Kruger and David Dunning, discovered that incompetent individuals, when compared with their more competent peers, tended to overestimate their ability and performance. In effect, they attempted to fill their skill gaps with an extra dose of bravado and braggadocio. Woody Allen once quipped, "Confidence is what you have before you understand the problem."

Just look around. In practically every arena, you will find leaders who, to the amazement of those closest to them, will deem themselves indisputably qualified, and will even go so far as to declare themselves best qualified for the role in question. However, for some unknown reason, only that individual sees this alleged abundance of skill, knowledge, and aptitude in him or herself. Others are left totally perplexed.

This stunning phenomenon, which psychologists call illusory superiority, is sweeping through every industry, every sector, and at every level. Illusory superiority is defined as a cognitive bias resulting in an individual's overestimation of his or her qualities and abilities, relative to others. Granted, the attitude isn't new, but the boldness and conviction with which it is displayed, and the numbers of individuals displaying this attitude, is unlike anything in recent memory. Subsequently, far too many leaders and would-be leaders are delusional, even hyper-delusional, in the assessments of their skills. These leaders are also equally delusional in the assessments of their impact, and the perceived high level of respect others hold for them.

So as not to be misunderstood, **a belief in one's self and a positive expectancy are, in fact, representative of a good and healthy mental state. However, when the belief is grossly incongruent with one's current level of performance or mastery, the results are rarely inspiring.** With all due respect to pop psych, thinking you can (one day) is a far cry from being able to perform it today.

The claim of leadership grossly misusing its imagination is far from mere conjecture, hyperbole, or sour grapes. Evidence of leaders' overestimation via self-perception, even exaggeration of skills and effectiveness, is plenteous. A study by The Korn Ferry Institute cited the results of a now classic poll in which 90% of the leaders surveyed believed themselves to be in the top 10% of performers. Needless to say, that is mathematically impossible, and it is also impossible to overestimate the impact this exaggerated sense of competence has on the bottom line of your organization. Steven Smith reported in his book entitled *Egonomics* that, 71% of businesspeople say that ego is costing their companies more than 15% of revenue per year.

Leaders must be learners. Leaders must be coachable. When a leader is of the opinion that he or she knows it all, adopting a "been there, done that" type of attitude, that leader stunts the growth and curiosity of those around them. This wouldn't be so bad if there were only a few leaders who were so overconfident in their ability to lead. Unfortunately, the number of overconfident leaders may outstrip the number of inquisitive growth-oriented leaders by an unimaginable order of magnitude. According to a survey conducted by Development Dimensions International (DDI) and reported in the Wall Street Journal, 72% of the 1,100 managers surveyed indicate they have never questioned their ability to be an effective leader. While that might sound reassuring, it really isn't. These individuals were asked to evaluate themselves in key leadership areas, and the overwhelming majority of responders rated themselves as "proficient" or "strong." However, when asked about their developmental needs, less than 15% identified *any* growth opportunities at all. It is then easy to conclude that if you don't think you have any growth opportunities, you make yourself extremely susceptible to the perils of overconfidence. DDI added that these results were consistent across a wide variety of business areas and functions.

While the leaders who struggle with imaginary competence attempt to rationalize their perceptions and conduct, the toll they extract within the organization is anything but imaginary. ***It really is a big deal if leaders believe themselves to be highly skilled***

and effective in interpersonal interactions, yet they continue to create a negative impact and outcomes. Their incongruence results in employees feeling disrespected, unappreciated, and underutilized. To say nothing of the heightened frustration of working for an ineffective, if not incompetent, leader. Consequently, these feelings and frustrations culminate in increased voluntary separations. As the adage goes, "People join organizations, but they leave leaders."

Turnover is expensive and is one of the added costs of leadership incompetence. Unfortunately, the list of costs doesn't stop at turnover. To that list, you must also add higher levels of employee disengagement and absenteeism. As if those issues weren't disconcerting enough, you also face lower levels of initiative and innovation. The greater cost of leadership incompetence is in the aggregate expense of squandered resources – both financial and human. Every leader should understand that to fall victim to a "runaway imagination" is extremely costly.

Here are 7 strategies to ensure you don't fall prey to an overzealous imagination regarding your leadership competence:

Muzzle Your Inner Critic. Take notice of your inner conversation. Note how you critique others. Are those critiques objective or a tool to compensate for your insecurities and fears? Pay close attention and seek balance and objectivity. You don't get better by tearing other people down.

Use Performance, Not Proclamations. Anyone can talk a good game, and your imagination is an expert at talking big. Train yourself to look at your performance as the measure of your current competence. After all, competence is about doing, not about overestimation, exaggeration, or empty proclamations.

Learn To Read The Metrics Of Success. Your leadership role comes complete with some hard metrics. They count, and shouldn't be ignored or minimized. It's very difficult to overestimate your competence when your success metrics continue to trend downward. Those hard metrics indicate where your current competencies match the demands of the role, and where there are clear opportunities for improvement. You may very well get better, but you can't claim or celebrate that level of competence until you achieve it.

Use 360° Feedback. Multi-sourced feedback is an excellent way to tame a sense of exaggerated competence. If you are hearing that you are deficient in specific areas of your role, and you are hearing that from multiple sources, it might be time for some candid introspection. 360° feedback can help to fill in many of the gaps common to biased self-assessments.

Commit To Continued Learning. Lifelong learning is a requirement of leadership. Staying engaged in the learning process assertively confronts notions of unsubstantiated competence in two very effective ways. First, it requires you to demonstrate what it is you say you have already mastered. Second, the learning process highlights how much more there is to learn about a topic.

Compete Internally, Collaborate Externally. This strategy is liberating. You are competing against your personal best, not your colleagues. Simply stated, if your personal best elevates you among your peers, so be it. But the team's mission is to accomplish a specific set of tasks in the most efficient and profitable manner possible. That requires collaboration.

Teach Others. Imaginary or exaggerated competence is no match for the curious mind of a student. An old maxim states that the best way to learn is to teach. I would add that the best way to discover what you don't know is to teach others. Teaching requires a facility with a topic that can't easily be faked. As such, teaching has a way of illuminating gaps in knowledge or awareness.

Strategies are powerful, but they are even more powerful when consistently and conscientiously executed. The above list of strategies is intended to be a starting point in reconciling your perceptions and your performance. Misalignment of the two can result in you residing in an imaginary world of your own making. You shouldn't be discouraged from having a positive self-image and high expectations, but you must avoid claiming a level of competence you have yet to obtain. To make that mistake is to misuse your (leadership) imagination.

The Temptations told a lovely and inspiring story in that classic hit "Just My Imagination." But that story was also a cautionary tale. One that every leader should heed – don't allow your imagination to run away with you.

Soulful Leadership Lesson: It was just your imagination! Many leaders are susceptible to an exaggerated sense of self-competence. However, their perception is totally uncorroborated by their performance. As tempting as it may be, it is detrimental to both the leader and the organization when leaders overestimate their skill sets. That hyper-confidence may serve you well in the breakroom when embellishing stories of high school pranks, but it plays thin in the boardroom and on the shop floor where you are expected to deliver "real" results.

Shakey Ground

9 Unconscious Biases That Place Workplace Relationships On Terra Tremulous

"While our biases may be unconscious, their existence is indisputable, and their consequences are undeniable."

Unconscious bias is real and can show up even in the highest ranks of an association, organization, even the White House. President Donald Trump is on record asserting that an Indiana-born judge, Gonzalo Curiel, could not be impartial, as President Trump put it, "because he's Mexican." Some believe the president's animus stems from Judge Curiel's role in a previous class-action lawsuit brought against Trump University for allegedly defrauding students.

The start of a brand-new work relationship is chock-full of challenges. The most significant of which are literally in the minds of the leader, the new hire, and the existing team members. Further complicating the challenge is the fact that none of the parties has a true clue as to how their initial and immediate perceptions become potential obstacles to an effective and productive relationship. To add further insult to injury, those perceptions and assessments transpire at lightning speed, and are not only unconscious but also often uncomplimentary. Because of these unconscious biases, the majority of work relationships start on terra tremulous, or shaky ground.

Given all of the unpredictability, uncertainty, and complexity surrounding initial perceptions, coupled with humanity's demonstrated propensity to be critically judgmental of differences and newcomers, only one Motown hit captures the nuanced impact of this cognitive cacophony. That song is the Temptations' 1974 hit "Shakey Ground." Categorically, "Shakey Ground" is the ideal song to characterize the mental dynamics accompanying the majority of workplace interactions.

A quote, initially printed in the Harvard Business Review, eloquently summarizes the challenges of unconscious bias in the workplace. Mahzarin Banaji, a social psychologist at Harvard, stated, "Most of us believe that we are ethical and unbiased. We imagine we're good decision makers, able to objectively size up a job candidate or a venture deal and reach a fair and rational conclusion that's in our, and our organization's best interests. But more than two decades of research confirms that, in reality, most of us fall woefully short of our inflated self-perception."

Unconscious bias is defined in many interesting and sometimes complicated ways. Yet, simply stated, unconscious bias refers to assumptions and conclusions formulated outside of our conscious awareness. These biases are the consequence of the brain making speedy judgments about situations and/or people. The judgments are themselves, an amalgamation of many varied elements.

Typically, these speedy judgments center on assumptions related to the other parties' physiological, psychological, professional, and peripheral status in comparison to how the assessor sees him or herself.

Most of us would say that such snap judgments are unfair and damaging. However, as it turns out, those snap judgments are also necessary. Researchers, such as those interviewed for the National Geographic Documentary titled LSD – Separating Myth from Molecule, state that at any given second we are bombarded by nearly 11 million pieces of information. Yet, our brains can process only 200 bits of the deluge at a time. Other scientists at MIT suggest the brain can only process 60 bits per second. Given the gross disparity between what is coming in and what is processed, there existed a need to extrapolate a larger meaning or significance from a rather minuscule sampling of data. To satisfy this need, we rely on "super-templates." These super templates or lightning quick assessments are in essence our unconscious biases.

Some early studies, such as those reported by Michael Solomon, Ph.D., Chairman, Marketing Department Graduate School of Business, NYU, suggested that within the first seven seconds of interacting with someone we have never met before, we make, on average, 11 judgments about that person. This practice is known as the 7-11 Rule.

To elaborate a bit more on the 7-11 Rule, when we are assessing an individual we think to be similar to how we see ourselves, generally speaking, we tend to be fairly objective, balanced, and accurate in our initial assessment. Conversely, the more different we perceive the other party to be from how we define ourselves, the more likely we are to lose that objectivity, balance, and accuracy. In general, with a few notable exceptions, difference tends to skew the initial assessment toward the negative.

If the 7-11 Rule shook you up a bit, then hold on tight, because recent research in the domain of neuroscience might feel like a 9.0 quake on the Richter scale. Neuro-researchers are now stating that as quickly as seven-one thousandths (.007) of a second, the brain acquires and amasses physical information about a stranger. Within another four-tenths (.4) of a second, a conclusion and a tentative course of action are formulated. That is lightning fast. By way of comparison and reference, all of this sampling and processing is happening in a time span that is roughly equivalent to half of a heartbeat.

Almost to a person, leaders scoff at the prospect of unconscious bias steering their decision-making processes and informing their perspectives of potential and performance. However, much to their chagrin, that is absolutely the case. In fact, it is quite commonplace to find decisions regarding personnel and/ or policy tainted by varying degrees of unconscious bias. No need to get defensive here. Actually, that may be why this topic is so sensitive and uncomfortable for so many leaders. Instead of becoming defensive, perhaps we should all become more determined to understand the challenge and work to minimize its impact. We must grasp that unconscious bias is a byproduct of cognitive processing. It is how the brain works. Yet, we must also grasp that while our biases may be unconscious, their existence is indisputable and their consequences are undeniable.

Unconscious biases may be unconscious, but they are far from being innocuous. In a very real sense, these unconscious biases are more than an inconvenience; they are extraordinarily expensive. Unconscious biases can alter the flow and direction of any process, and in some cases, our unconscious biases are life-threatening. This is true whether that process is the course of an NBA basketball game, the type of prescription and follow-up care you receive from a doctor, the odds of securing a job interview, the objectivity of your performance review, or the trajectory of a career.

As appalling as it may sound, imagine going to the ER with classic symptoms of a heart attack – to include chest pain, nausea, sweating, and pain radiating down your left arm - only to be misdiagnosed as having indigestion and then sent home. Because of systemic unconscious bias in the health care system, women are statistically less likely to be taken seriously regarding symptoms of a heart attack. Data suggests that the misdiagnosis of a heart attack occurs 50% more often for women than for men. This was exactly Carolyn Thomas' experience. And sadly, her story is not as unique as it ought to be. In many ways, Carolyn was "lucky." British researchers reported that for women whose heart attacks are not diagnosed, those women are 70% more likely to die.

African American patients face similar challenges in the health care system. National Medical Association president Dr. Albert Morris shared with ABC News, "It has been demonstrated multiple times in the past that whites receive better care and get care sooner than their African-American counterparts." Research published in the Journal of General Internal Medicine, conducted by The Disparities Solutions Center, affiliated with Harvard University and Massachusetts General Hospital, found that unconscious bias can affect how doctors diagnose and treat patients, consequentially resulting in inferior care for African American patients.

Examples of unconscious bias affecting African American patients are ubiquitous. For example, numerous published studies show that pain prescriptions for African American patients differ in type and duration than white patients with the identical diagnosis. Not only are there disparities in prescriptions, but African Americans are also less likely to receive referrals for advanced cardiac care.

Would you find it interesting to know that research, conducted by University of Pennsylvania assistant professor, Justin Wolfers, and Cornell graduate student, Joseph Price, uncovered a very interesting pattern in how NBA referees officiated games? The study discovered that the race of the referee played a role in how many fouls the ref called and on whom. White referees called fouls at a higher rate against Black players than against White players. The study also found that Black officials called fouls more frequently against White players than Black, but noted that this tendency was not as prominent as among White referees. According to the principal researchers, this disparity in referees' behavior was potentially obstructive. Here is the potential impact: an all-White team would, given all other variables are held equal, win two extra games over the course of an 82-game season. That potentially translates to the difference between being in the playoffs and watching the playoffs from the comfort of your couch.

Of course, the referees are human. And I am sure it is fair to say that the overwhelming majority of refs harbored no conscious malice or ill will against any player based solely on the player's race. In fact, if asked individually, each ref, I am sure, would tell us exactly that. However, the data establish a clear pattern of bias.

The tendency to assess and assume is primal. This conversation is not aimed at eradicating the practice (a futile endeavor), but instead to avoid becoming a prisoner of the practice. It is true that assumptions are going to occur; the key is to seek more balance of perception in your initial encounter and during your initial interaction. This should become the intentional pursuit of every leader.

You might think that big-time celebrities or dignitaries are shielded from such unfair and humiliating experiences. Think again. You need only ask Eric Holder, Marlee Beth Matlin, Peter Dinklage, Oprah Winfrey, John Goodman, Charles Belk, Ellen DeGeneres, Tony Cox, or Betty White, and the list continues ad infinitum. Each of these individuals had to contend with and conquer various types of biases.

Google had an epiphany, of sorts, regarding unconscious bias in software design. It turns out that an unconscious bias for right-handedness afflicted the iOS YouTube app. Consequently, when left-handed users recorded video in the landscape orientation, once uploaded, the video would play upside-down.

From these examples and practically countless others, every leader should remember, if you have unmanaged assumptions or biases, they will surface somewhere in the decision-making process.

The topic of unconscious bias is gaining more attention and coming to the forefront of leadership conversations more and more often today. In many cases, it is the focal point of the discussion - and rightfully so. The consequences of unconscious bias have a direct impact on the organizational bottom line. It is time to stop denying the existence of unconscious bias and seek a deeper understanding of its operation and consequences.

Consider the organizational impact of using the name on the resume to screen out candidates. Consider the impact of granting leadership opportunities based on the height of the candidate. Consider the impact of gender influencing the objectivity of performance reviews and talent assessments. Consider the impact of an assumption of intelligence (or absence thereof) contingent upon the candidates' degree of attractiveness. What is the impact of assuming, categorically, that men are better leaders than women? All of those seemingly hypothetical scenarios are real and documented examples of forms of unconscious bias. Furthermore, a plethora of research establishes that these biases, and many others, are prevalent in today's workforce. It is very difficult to imagine that an environment inundated by such bias, and in which such bias is ignored, would be the ideal environment for the establishment and furtherance of a healthy and thriving enterprise.

When left unchecked, unconscious bias can turn the workplace into a daunting obstacle course. Leaders who are impaired by unconscious bias impede the effective and efficient leveraging of human capital. Stated simply and directly, unconscious bias creates impediments to two prime directives of leadership. The first directive is to develop and maintain a respectful and inclusive environment, conducive to the growth and development of talented individuals. The second directive is to ensure the best match of talent to task. Unconscious bias stands in direct and active opposition to these fundamental goals.

Social scientists, neuroscientists, and academicians have assembled an ever-expanding catalog of biases. The catalog's subset of more than 200 biases dealing specifically with decision-making, belief, and behavioral biases can be sliced and diced a multiplicity of ways, but nine biases are of particular importance to you as a leader in a diverse, dynamic, and demanding global marketplace.

1. **Blind Spot Bias**. As the title implies, this bias involves a blind spot – specifically, the leader's inability to see his or her preconceptions, prejudices, and partialities. With blind spot bias, the leader is limited in identifying his or her bias, but thinks he or she is skilled at identifying those challenges in others. Additionally, with a blind spot bias, the leader firmly believes he or she is less biased than are others.

2. **Affinity Bias**. This bias reflects the leader's propensity to find greater comfort in interacting with those he or she shares commonalities of import. The leader arbitrarily assigns the degree of significance associated with any specific element of commonality. Traditionally, such elements influential in affinity bias include race, gender, alma mater, politics, and the like. Because of the leader's heightened comfortability, select individuals reap advantages in the form of increased informal development, higher exposure, and more aggressive advocacy.

3. **Confirmation Bias**. Confirmation bias is the tendency to look for evidence to substantiate your perceptions and expectations, while simultaneously overlooking or minimizing contradictory data. This bias also extends to the leader's interpretation of data and the recollection of events.

4. **Attractiveness Bias**. This bias is present when a leader assumes, ever so irrationally, that "attractive" people are more bountifully endowed with the most desirable personal and professional traits. This bias results in the leader thinking the more attractive candidates or associates are smarter, more creative, more talented, more skilled, and by extrapolation – more promotable.

5. **Outgroup Homogeneity Bias**. As a result of this bias, a leader believes groups with which he or she self-identifies are more diverse and varied than other groups. For his or her self-identifying groups, the leader can apply a granular perspective and finds it much easier to acknowledge individualism. In

contrast, any group with which the leader does not self-identify is consistently viewed superficially and monolithically.

6. **Attribution Bias**. Attribution bias manifests in how the leader imputes causality to events and outcomes. The attribution is formulated, in large part, on limited information and incomplete evidence. Consequently, the attribution is often inaccurate. In one variance of attribution bias, the leader's conclusions are driven by an assessment of the character or motives of an individual, without considering how external drivers contributed to the way a particular event unfolded.

7. **Conformity Bias**. The inclination to acquiesce to the opinions and mimic the behaviors of others in a group. This bias results in suppressing of insights, in spite of strongly believing his or her position to be ostensibly correct and a better option than the course of action adopted by the team.

8. **Selective Perception**. A tendency to notice and note behaviors insofar as those behaviors reinforce the leader's preconceptions, prejudices, or partialities. Additionally, this bias impairs the leader's ability to notice and note the identical behavior in groups for whom the leader fails to hold a similar expectation.

9. **Contrast Effect**. A phenomenon by which the leader's assessment sways either favorably or unfavorably based on the sequence in which data is presented. Of particular concern is that the leader's assessment is actually independent of the objective success criteria of the job. Instead, the assessment is based on how the current candidate or idea compares or contrasts to the one most recently presented.

Unfortunately, these nine biases are rampant in every type of organizational structure. While their presence may be ubiquitous, there is little awareness of their presence and even less commitment on behalf of many leaders to rooting these biases out. Clearly, if little to no attention is directed to this challenge, it is fair to say that relationships and results will struggle to find a firm foundation upon which to build. Under these conditions, terra tremulous instead of terra firma will remain the organizational norm. That is a shaky proposition, indeed.

Here are 5 ways to firm up the foundation of your work relationships:

1. **Accept Unconscious Bias As A Reality**. The research pertaining to unconscious bias is quite impressive and thoroughly conclusive. And with that, there is no good reason to continue to deny its potential influence on your previous people and policy decisions. Accept the fact. Then resolve not to allow unconscious biases to highjack your leadership effectiveness going forward.

2. **Pay Attention To Your Surprise**. Surprise is a gift. When you find yourself surprised as a result of interacting with someone, that surprise is the gateway to identifying your unconscious bias. Obviously, their skill set, knowledge base, or experiences were not as you expected. The question is why didn't you expect it? Pondering that question is assuredly a step in the right direction.

3. **Educate Your Team**. The entire team needs in-depth education and training on the concept of unconscious bias in order to effect meaningful change in the culture. Provide your team opportunities to learn about the concept, the consequences, and strategies to combat unconscious bias.

4. **Encourage Open Dialogue**. Encourage others to speak up, and out, regarding their perspectives and experiences. Specifically, ask them about any "patterns" of bias they may have observed in decisions or interactions. Such discourse is an excellent way to evaluate the alignment of your intentions

and impact. Open dialogue can help you discover patterns to which you are currently blind.

5. **Invest In Expanding Your Bubble**. Many unconscious biases are nurtured by isolation and ignorance. Invest in learning more about the world around you. Read different blogs and books outside your usual selections. Pick an issue and explore the other side. Listen to different music. Watch a different genre of shows and movies. Most importantly, talk to people who hold different views and perspectives.

In today's workplace, too many employees are singing The Temptations' hit - "Shakey Ground." The foundation of their work relationship is quaking, and the footing along their career path is becoming increasingly precarious as a consequence of unconscious biases. We should be ever mindful that what is true in architecture is also true in work relationships; it is very difficult to build something significant and sustainable on a shaky foundation.

Soulful Leadership Lesson: Unconscious bias is real, and very real in its consequences. In fact, due to unconscious biases, most workplace relationships struggle initially to find sure footing. Sadly, many relationships never mature to more solid and stable footing. Every leader should understand that it is irresponsible and cowardly to allow personal biases, prejudices, or preferences to masquerade as objectivity. Moreover, your employees are not fooled in the least. Invest in identifying and managing your unconscious biases, and you may find yourself achieving some rather uncommon results.

Quicksand

7 Behaviors Keeping Leaders Mired In The Quicksand Of Accountability Avoidance And How To Escape

"Show me an organization in which accountability avoidance is the norm, and I'll show you an organization in which the actualization of the mission and values will remain troublingly elusive."

Today's headlines are replete with example after example of a lack of accountability. This is particularly obvious regarding serious misconduct by members of the C-Suite and board members. Too many, in positions of responsibility, opted to turn a blinded eye to Theranos' medical and financial performance issues, United Healthcare's False Claims Act problems, or Wells Fargo's deceptive and fraudulent practices. These examples and countless others are illustrative of the consequences of accountability avoidance at every level of the organization.

If I say the word quicksand, what immediately comes to mind? Danger? Trouble? Fear? Undoubtedly, there is a great deal of myth, misconception, and misunderstanding associated with the geological anomaly known as quicksand.

Legends abound regarding the fate of many an unsuspecting sojourner who unfortunately found himself or herself hopelessly trapped in a menacing and unforgiving pit of quicksand. Horror stories, science fiction movies, and even run-of-the-mill adventure flicks are full of scenarios in which quicksand elevates the suspense of a scene. Odds are you are thinking of an example right now. So that begs the question, what is quicksand anyway?

Quicksand, as defined at www.EpicWildlife.com, is a colloid hydrogel consisting of fine granular material (such as sand, silt, or clay) and water. When left undisturbed, its surface gives the impression of being solid. However, that is only an illusion. When as little as 1% of pressure is applied, the surface immediately liquefies and is incapable of bearing weight. Consequently, the object breaking the surface (human or animal) sinks in direct proportion to its density.

The real threat of quicksand is not total submersion; instead, the real threat is related to the extreme difficulty of freeing yourself from its herculean grasp. I'm sure we can agree – a pit of quicksand isn't to be trifled with.

Apparently, Martha and the Vandellas had an awareness and appreciation for the dangers of quicksand – particularly the threat of ensnarement. Their awareness is evident as the group sings of how a lover's soft touch and gentle kiss gradually pulls a muse deeper and deeper in love until finally the muse is wholly and entirely engulfed.

Martha and the Vandellas' 1963 hit, "Quicksand," is a great allegory to remind leaders of the importance of a key aspect of leadership. While being ensnared and entangled in a quagmire of amorous passions isn't a daily concern for most leaders, there should be, however, concern regarding the consequences arising from an absence of accountability skills. When it comes to the perpetual ignoring of disruptive and counterproductive behaviors, I hear Martha and the Vandellas bellowing a warning to every leader – Beware, Quicksand!

Accountability is one of those peculiar concepts that every leader agrees is important, but it is a skill at which few leaders excel. Often when leaders are confronted regarding obvious deficiencies in this area, a leap toward defensiveness is more the norm than not. The excuses offered for their procrastination or out-and-out avoidance are innumerable and incredibly imaginative. However, as you already know, very few of your colleagues, direct reports, and key stakeholders regard an excuse as being synonymous with a solution.

What is accountability? If you consider the first portion of the word, it is easy to understand what accountability really means. To account for or reckon is to assess how something measures up to a goal or a standard. To hold someone accountable is to assess how well their performance aligned with their promise, how their conduct facilitated the fulfillment of the contract, or how accurately their deliverables aligned with their declarations. Often, at home and work, there is a marked difference between our expectations and what we actually experience.

In the context of the day-to-day responsibilities of leadership, ***accountability is a process by which an individual learns how his or her actions fall short of the expectations or standards***

held for a task or set of tasks. As straightforward as that definition is, so too is the process of holding others accountable when exercised in a timely and constructive manner. Sadly, far too many leaders procrastinate in initiating these vitally important conversations. As a result of this tendency to procrastinate, the cache of nightmarish stories of accountability conversations gone wild seems only to enlarge with each passing day.

When leaders neglect their responsibility to hold individuals accountable, it is a fact that nothing of lasting good or benefit results from such a decision. In a misguided attempt to be "friendly," the leader ignores the early warning signs of problematic behavior or performance. This impudent decision opens the door to a vast array of new challenges. Finally, the leader awakes to the magnitude of the problem only to discover him or herself so deeply mired that the situation appears hopeless. Just as if trapped in an unrelenting pool of quicksand, the leader struggles and struggles only to sink deeper into dysfunction and ineffectiveness.

If the consequences are so devastating, why do so many leaders avoid initiating accountability conversations, or at least avoid initiating the conversation until they find themselves on the brink of pandemonium and disaster? There may be many contributing factors at work in this situation, some working independently while others work concurrently, all resulting in a state of affairs that is, at best, suboptimal and destined to accelerate in a downward spiral. A listing of the seven key contributing factors, or as I refer to them, the seven pits, includes the following:

Pit #1 Insufficient Courage. If you understand courage to be, as defined by Merriam-Webster, the mental or moral strength to venture, persevere, and withstand danger, fear, or difficulty, then at the root of accountability avoidance is the leader's lack of courage.

There is no way around this. The requisite courage is birthed of the leader's passion for excellence, commitment to those in his or her direct report, and a conviction to lead by example. Leading by example includes proactively addressing what needs addressing - in a constructive manner. You can count on this: where there is insufficient courage, accountability conversations are assuredly infrequent, ambiguous, and unproductive.

Pit #2 Waiting For The Perfect Time. One of the common obstacles to delivering a timely accountability message is the myth that there is a "perfect time" to engage an associate. I firmly subscribe to the philosophy that the closer to the occurrence you deliver the feedback, the greater the probability of the change in behavior. A "good time" is such a time as when the associate can receive and process the content of the conversation. In this regard, getting it done is better than trying to get it perfect. Waiting for the perfect time can turn into, "The time just never seemed ideal to bring it up."

Pit #3 Mistakenly Valuing Popularity Over Productivity. The desire to "be liked" is a powerful motivator. Unfortunately, that desire can cloud your leadership judgment. That clouded judgment, in the moment, suggests to you that ignoring poor performance or other misconduct is the right call. Doing so is usually a mistake. By electing not to confront the behavior, you reason that you are safeguarding your likeability among your direct reports. The truth of the matter is that your direct reports will not only like you more, but will respect you more when you fulfill the demands of your role. That includes proactively and constructively holding them accountable. ***It is a poor trade-off to prize popularity over productivity.***

Pit #4 Fear Of Short-Term Demotivation. A top priority of effective leadership is to encourage growth and development. This priority requires that you – the leader – both cheerlead and correct. While the ratio of cheerleading to correction may vary for each associate, the fact remains that significant and substantive improvement requires accountability. If you fear that an accountability conversation will put an associate into a short-term funk, just consider how funky their attitude might become once they finally learn that they have been falling short of expectations for an extended period – and you neglected to inform them? Granted, a short-term dip in performance is a possibility, but that dip is much easier from which to recover than it is to correct the consequences of an extended period of half-truths and placation.

Pit #5 Questioning Your Preparation. The uncertainty surrounding how to facilitate a constructive accountability conversation is more than enough to paralyze many leaders. When you are feeling somewhat confused and frustrated by your lack of confidence, even the thought of attempting to hold an associate accountable can create feelings ranging from moderately uncomfortable to intensely frazzled. Without a template to help guide you through the conversation, it is less than likely that anything productive will transpire. A good template is a lifeline for a leader trapped in the quicksand of accountability avoidance.

Pit #6 Fear Of A Nuclear Reaction. How an individual might react when called into account is, admittedly, unpredictable. During the conversation, emotions can run high, and the dynamics can quickly get far out of hand. Of course, none of us gleefully looks forward to outbursts of yelling, fist pounding, or weeping while attempting to facilitate an accountability conversation. In light of the possibility of a worst-case outcome, you might reason that avoiding the conversation is the wisest alternative. Yet, in reality, you are only slipping deeper and deeper in the quicksand of avoidance. Additionally, if there did exist a threat of emotional outburst, your procrastination only adds fuel for a potentially larger emotional (nuclear) reaction.

Pit #7 Masking Personal Culpability. You might find yourself procrastinating in holding others accountable if you feel partially at fault in the creation of the situation in question. The source of your concerns could range from failing to set clear expectations, to failing to provide the required resources, or simply allowing the interpersonal dynamics to grow progressively disruptive. Whatever the outward situation, you know in your heart of hearts that, as a leader, you failed your team. Anticipating their scathing and merited indictment, and the resulting humiliation, you find it easier to continue to tolerate the unacceptable behavior than address it. Unfortunately, this scenario produces no winners. All parties involved, as well as those on the periphery, continue to sink deeper and deeper in the voracious quicksand of accountability avoidance.

As I share the list of seven "pits" with leaders, they usually know someone ensnared in one or more of the pits. Interestingly, their comments emphasize how accurately the pit describes someone else's situation, but rarely their own. Perhaps you had a similar experience as you read the list. While the list is a powerful tool for coaching others, its primary intention is to facilitate personal introspection. With that said, which of your behaviors did you find represented among the seven pits? There is a popular saying in the medical profession that seems most apropos, "Diagnosis is half of the cure."

What if you had a way to circumvent the hazardous pits of accountability avoidance? What if you had a way to diminish the probability of creating and perpetuating the consequences of accountability avoidance? What if you had a causeway to span over the pits and perils of accountability avoidance? What if…? For many leaders, in today's fast-paced and dynamic environments, lustfully pondering "What if" is as good as it gets. Fortunately, you don't have to relegate your effectiveness to an empty and aimless "what if." There is a real and viable solution to the challenges and consequences associated with accountability avoidance. The solution is in mastering a simple but powerful tool - the ARC-D Accountability Dialogue Model™.

Let's delve into each component.

A - Actions. Because actions are observable, you want to point out the action or behavior deemed undesirable, unacceptable, or inappropriate. A conversation about a concrete event is much easier to facilitate than one referencing a nebulous or ethereal issue such as an attitude or attempting to substantiate the legitimacy of an imputed motive.

Positioning the associate's questionable action prominently at the start of the conversation helps to clarify the purpose of the dialogue and to communicate the gravity of the situation.

When presenting the action, strive to be as objective in your reporting as possible. This is achieved by resisting the temptation to use incendiary labels. By labeling the associate's actions as rude, crude, inconsiderate, unprofessional, etc. you have essentially opened the door to a potentially heated debate. Mind you; the ensuring debate won't focus on whether or not the action actually occurred, instead it is a debate as to whether you mislabeled or mischaracterized the associate's behavior. Many an accountability conversation has been derailed by this simple, and easily avoidable, mistake.

Component Example:

Eschew   *"Jan, the attitude you displayed in the meeting this morning was insanely inappropriate and entirely unacceptable. Let's get one thing straight, as long as I am your supervisor, we will never, ever, experience that attitude again. Am I clear?"*

Emulate   *"Jan, the specific observation I'd like to share with you centers on the action of putting your feet up on the table during the CEO's briefing this morning and referring to him as the spawn of Chuckie and the source of all lies."*

R - Result. This component emphasizes what transpired in the wake of the action. Its focus is rearward. Your aim at this juncture is to articulate the percipient impact and collateral damage resulting from the associate's misconduct or unacceptable performance. The "Result" discussion can address the emotional impact as well as the physical outcomes of the undesired action. For most leaders, the "Result" of the undesired action is the catalyst to initiate an accountability conversation.

As you move through the process of holding an associate accountable, you must be especially clear when articulating the adverse impact of their behavior to date. You will need to speak directly to the behavior's impact on the team's dynamics, trust, meeting of deadlines, or any process or outcome the associate's actions adversely influenced.

You may find the associate becomes defensive at this point and desires to promote the intention of their actions over the actual impact they created. This is not the time to get into a debate over the associate's intentions. Often you will hear, "I didn't mean for that to happen." And while that may be true, it doesn't absolve the associate of his or her accountability for the resulting outcomes. It falls to you to help the associate thoroughly understand the difference between intent and impact. If the impact is unfavorable, you must address the action that precipitated that unfavorable impact.

Remember, some individuals are motivated to change their behavior because of how they have impaired, impeded, or inconvenienced others. However, other individuals are motivated to change their behaviors because of the future consequences to them if they don't make the requested changes.

Component Example:

Eschew   *"Because of you, everything is all screwed up. On top of that, the CEO wants to talk to me about your contentious and contemptible attitude. I am thoroughly pissed to have to deal with you, your mess, and your nonsense."*

Emulate   *"Let me share with you the result of your actions. Our team, as a whole, wasn't viewed in a favorable light. But you particularly have earned a label of being disrespectful. I am personally disappointed by your actions. Moreover, our team is no longer in the running to steward the Reynolds project. As you might have noticed, our team dynamic is now strained."*

C - Consequences. In this model, consequence speaks to how you will address what has already transpired, and what will occur if the associate's behavior were to continue uncorrected.

At this point in the accountability process, you impress upon the associate that any further display of his or her previous undesired actions will not be tolerated. Again, this message must be explicit and direct. Your goal is to ensure the associate understands that continuance of the identified behavior or any similar behaviors will meet with disciplinary consequences.

The consequence for the present delinquency and any future shortcomings can take a multiplicity of forms. Consequences might consist of censure, reprimand, or punishment such as revocation of privileges, reassignment, suspension, and even termination. Of course, the sternness of the corrective action is contingent upon the severity of the misconduct; coupled with the number of previous conversations you have had in an attempt to rectify the issue.

To be most effective, the consequences must be impacting. This means the disciplinary action must have ramifications in an area of importance and significance to the associate.

It is worth reiterating that the consequences should be proportional to the scale and significance of the offense. Being either too harsh with the associate or too lenient is equally counterproductive and ineffective.

Component Example:

Eschew   *"That was idiotic, irresponsible, and just plain lame. Just don't talk to me right now, don't even look at me. I can't believe I put you in charge of this project, and you decide to act like a child. Fine, I'll treat you like a child. Get out of my office."*

Emulate   *"As a consequence, you will not attend the industry trade show in Honolulu, nor will you be a member of the project task force next month. If this behavior or similar behaviors were to continue, you would be subject to suspension or even termination.*

D - Desired Behavior. How well you facilitate this component will have a direct bearing on how the associate feels about the exchange. You want the associate to feel empowered to make changes, not merely left feeling criticized. When you provide clear recommendations on what behaviors or actions must replace the old behavior – in essence, a map to improvement - even the most critical of observations are understood as personal assistance instead of a personal attack.

What applies to each of the other components of the ARC-D Accountability Dialogue Model™ is especially true with the Desired Behavior component - clarity is crucial. In this component, you want to present the new behavioral expectations by clearly laying out what your expectations are moving forward. In essence, you are outlining and entering into a new behavioral contract between yourself and your direct report.

The associate should have a clear understanding of what course of action is acceptable if he or she encounters a set of circumstances similar to those outlined in the accountability dialogue. It is well worth an investment of time and effort to rectify any confusion before you conclude this conversation, so don't be in a rush. If the associate leaves the conversation confused, there is little chance of a change in his or her behavior.

When it comes to the style and tone with which you present the desired behaviors, you have a great deal of latitude. You will need to decide whether you wish the exchange to be a monologue or a free-flowing dialogue. As a rule, the more egregious the incident, the more assertive, directive, and prescriptive your presentation of the desired behaviors. For those situations that are less offensive, you may choose to employ a consultative approach in exploring the best strategies to prevent a reoccurrence of the problematic circumstances. Each approach is effective, when matched to the appropriate set of conditions and weighed against the severity of the situation.

There are several useful communication techniques to gage the associate's true comprehension of the expected new standard of conduct. You may opt to have the associate articulate what is unacceptable behavior, and why it is such. Then have the associate offer his or her understanding of the new expectations. This paraphrasing technique can unmask areas of uncertainty.

A succinct and clear message, including recommendations on how to improve, is almost certainly better received than a message laced with venomous criticism.

Component Example:

Eschew   *"So, here's what you will not do. You will never behave like that again. In fact, it will never cross your mind that such behavior is even an option. Because it isn't. Get it together, now! If not, I will be forced to help you find a new mailing address. Do you understand the words that are coming out of my mouth?"*

Emulate   *"As a future desired behavior, I'll ask you to be mindful of our organizational values as you express your opinion. It is my expectation that you will adopt behavior consistent with our pledge and commitment to respect. What questions do you have concerning this expectation?"*

The ARC-D Accountability Dialogue Model™ is a highly effective and extremely valuable template for initiating and facilitating constructive accountability dialogues. It is clearly a wise way to navigate around the menacing pits of quicksand waiting to ensnare you and other leaders in the quagmire of accountability avoidance.

As you master each component of the model, your confidence and competence are sure to soar. As that occurs, you can also expect to see critical business metrics within your sphere of influence do likewise.

I doubt that Martha and the Vandellas were thinking of accountability avoidance as they performed their 1960's hit, but it turns out, they were offering leaders very sound advice - avoid the quicksand at all cost.

Soulful Leadership Lesson: There is, perhaps, no other leadership skill deficiency that reverberates so widely and as loudly as accountability avoidance. The toll it extracts on productivity and profitability is almost incalculable. To add insult to injury, freeing yourself of the misconceptions and irrationality surrounding accountability avoidance is tantamount to attempting to free yourself from the unrelenting grasp of quicksand. Luckily, there is a lifeline available in the form of the ARC-D model™.

What's Goin' On

Why Poor Communicators Are A Detriment To Your Organization

"The problems created by poor communication result in conditions antithetical to the organizational goals and objectives."

The hope was to make things better, but that wasn't the impact. After a horrific incident, in which a passenger on a United Airlines flight, was brutally dragged through the aisle and evicted from an overbooked flight from Chicago O'Hare to Louisville, CEO Oscar Munoz made a statement about the situation. Unfortunately, Munoz's reaction was neither timely nor empathetic. For the CEO to characterize the incident as a "re-accommodation" clearly missed the mark and made an unconscionable situation even tenser. His choice of words and defensive tone actually served to further fuel the public outcry. The fallout was immediate.

In 1971, Marvin Gaye challenged our consciences and our hearts as he offered a stirring commentary on the societal and environmental issues of his day. While Marvin questioned the direction and uprightness of politics, government, economics, and community, today employees in organizations around the globe ask their version of Marvin's timeless question. However, these employees are specifically asking regarding the dysfunction in their team dynamics and their uncertainty concerning organizational direction. Yes, it is true; associates, team members, and colleagues are asking their leaders - "What's goin' on?" Even more importantly, they are expecting their leaders to provide answers.

As reported by numerous studies and surveys, one of the lingering sources of frustration, exclusion, and employee dissatisfaction is poor communication between leaders and employees. Poor communication can be understood from a number of different perspectives, but what is singular by way of consequence is that poor communication adversely impacts every business success metric important to growth, image, and viability.

If people are left wondering what actions you expect of them, then the likelihood of creating market-expanding results is ridiculously improbable. Confusing or ambiguous messaging is clearly not a strength platform, but these confusing messages are both commonplace and costly. HR Magazine reports that in a survey of 4,000 employees, 46% said they routinely received confusing or unclear directions, with 36% of these employees reporting it happening up to three times each day. Participants in the study estimated they wasted about 40 minutes of productivity each day trying to interpret unclear or confusing directions.

The threats of poor communication and the resulting masses of poorly informed employees are very real. It is foolish to argue otherwise. However, the benefits of communicating in a consistent and candid manner are equally as real, and available, if you are willing to invest the energy and discipline to harvest those benefits. A Towers Watson study concludes that companies with highly effective communication practices enjoy 47% higher total returns to shareholders compared with firms that are least effective at communicating. If you need a little more motivation to enhance the effectiveness of your communications, here's another interesting point from the Towers Watson study - top communicating companies experience some 30% higher market valuation compared with their poorer communicating counterparts. By now, it should be painfully obvious that **communicating effectively pays handsome dividends while communicating ineffectively extracts a king's ransom from your company's coffers.**

It is perhaps leadership's well-documented propensity for erratically sharing information, and that information routinely being of such poor quality, that gave rise to the colloquialism the Mushroom Effect. I can remember early in my work experience hearing some of the older employees say, "Management treats us like mushrooms. They just keep us in the dark and feed us… uhm, uhm, …manure." As some of you know, there is another term used in the original statement for which I substituted the word manure. Nonetheless, it would appear that the mushroom effect is alive, and sadly, according to many employees, proliferating.

Censuswide, a consulting group in the UK, and Geckoboard, a KPI dashboard software firm, shared results of their recent study entitled Mushroom Management. The findings were enlightening as they highlighted the need for improved communication. Their study showed that more than 4 out of 5 employees surveyed wanted to hear more frequently from their leaders about how their company was doing. Their report also showed that more than 90% of employees surveyed said they would rather hear bad news than no news. This pattern of poor or non-communication between leaders and employees is a self-defeating practice. Again, it just seems impractical to expect people to bring their best solutions to the table when they don't have timely and accurate information with which to analyze the problem at hand.

As you attempt to lead your organization, the more often your employees have to ask themselves, "What's goin' on," the more slippery grows your grip on respect, credibility, and influence. It stands to reason that a steady diet of misinformation, disinformation, or no information at all will leave the leader-employee relationship astoundingly malnourished. Just how effective can you hope to be if your employees don't respect you, don't trust you, nor do you hold sway in any way over what they chose to do? Such a situation is the true epitome of titular leadership.

Of course, communicating consistently and effectively can be challenging even under "normal" conditions, but modern leaders face an added level of complexity in today's swift and dynamic marketplace - fast-paced, large-scale change.

Given that most organizations are in some stage of a change cycle, the need for ongoing communication - timely and accurate - is paramount. Referring back to the Censuswide and Geckoboard study, their research found that only 10% of employees surveyed were aware of their company's progress in real time. Allow me to translate that factoid. Ninety percent of employees don't know how well or how poorly the company is doing toward achieving its transformational goals. Unbelievable! Dealing with change is hard enough; expecting people to accept and embrace change, of any sort, type, or size, without continuous and timely information is just insanely arrogant. No wonder people are looking around, scratching their heads, and asking, "What's goin' on?"

When associates feel left out of the loop, they soon begin to leave their motivation, creativity, focus, and drive at home, instead of leveraging those vital assets in the workplace. That is if you are lucky enough to get them to come to work at all. Poor communication can be both frustrating and stressful. An inter-company study conduct by Watson Wyatt found that differences in leader-to-direct report communications practices were directly responsible for an 18% variation in absenteeism rates. That figure is stunning, but the loss production, the additional stress, and forfeited profitability are even more mind-blowing.

Absenteeism is one thing, but turnover is quite another. If you prove yourself to be an ineffective communicator, you may soon have no one with whom to speak. Watson Wyatt found that organizations with effective communication practices were more than 50% more likely to report employee turnover levels below the industry average. Who knew? ***If you master the art of keeping people informed, you also master the art of keeping people in the organization.*** That's right; communication is just that powerful. This important fact was corroborated by the Censuswide and Geckobaord study that shows that 1 in 4 employees surveyed has quit, or knows someone who has quit, due to a lack of transparency and communication in the workplace. ***No organization can expect to successfully compete in today's competitive marketplace while simultaneously hobbling itself through practices and patterns of poor communication.***

Every leader knows that high absenteeism and high turnover are undesirable outcomes, what every leader may not know is the degree to which his or her style and pattern of communication contributes to the cultivation and manifestation of those undesired outcomes. Many leaders feign to be concerned, but few seem truly committed to preventing these undesirable, but preventable, outcomes from ravishing their organizational productivity and profitability. It takes a great deal more than a worried expression or a troubled countenance to address this challenge.

The weaker, insecure, and ineffective leader often chooses to hide behind "need to know policies." Citing these policies as the reason for the sketchy information shared with his or her direct reports. Surely, there is a place for such policies, and surely, there is information that is of a sensitive and private nature, but everything can't be "Top Secret." When possible, share what you can, and do so as timely as you can, in order to keep your associates fully engaged. Your commitment to sharing in a timely fashion need not waiver whether the news is good or bad.

It is irrational and unjust to expect employees to be active, participating members of "self-directed" teams, to be proactively engaged in decision-making and solution creation if they don't have the latest and most accurate information with which to work. If they can't do their jobs, soon you won't have a job.

In much the same way that a vocal performer's voice may crack under the strain and stress of a pressure-packed performance, an insecure leader will falter in his or her communication strategy and execution. Pressure has a way of revealing imperfections and defects. One utterly debilitating defect for some leaders is the fear of being eclipsed by their direct reports. So, as a defense against this perceived threat, these leaders stonewall and refuse to share any information of true import or consequence.

I am in no way attempting to justify the practice of stonewalling associates, our life experiences have shown us that insecurity can prompt many ineffective behaviors. It appears, at least when it comes to the sharing of information, the insecure and the inept leader may have a good reason for consternation. Research validates that if associates are provided the same information as the leader, with an explanation of all circumstances and constraints, the associates will make a decision of similar quality to that of the leader. Being cognizant of this fact, out of a twisted interpretation of self-preservation, insecure leaders opt to dispense only a minimum amount of information, and they do that begrudgingly. Again, their unexpressed goal is to create job security, but that, of course, is only an illusion. With each reluctantly wrung drop of information, the employees' frustrations escalate. Whether this practice is a conscious strategy on behalf of these leaders to keep their direct reports in the dark, or an unconscious default approach, it is a highly ineffective way to lead.

Still, even today, there are leaders who believe that hoarding information makes them important and powerful. They think of themselves as the gatekeepers of wisdom and the turnstiles of knowledge. Wrong. What hoarding and rationing information really makes them is a corporate liability and culturally undesirable. If information is power, then the results created via sharing timely and accurate information with eager problem solvers is even more powerful. Employees don't want to be rationed out bits and pieces of information in accordance with what the leader thinks they can handle. Remember they are adults also. If you really want to empower your team and fully leverage their innovative talents and skills, keep them updated and oriented with the latest information.

In retail, hospitality, health care or transportation, any day of the week, you can hear, "Lady, I don't know, I just work here. Nobody ever tells me anything." Change the words, change the industry, but the sentiment rings familiar. As disconcerting as that is, such comments aren't limited to the front lines. This discontent and disinterest permeate all levels of organizations. It isn't difficult to find members of the leadership hierarchy who utter the same words as those of the front-line employees. If the leaders don't know what is going on, how can they inform the employees? Moreover, the bigger question is if the leadership doesn't know what is going on who does?

It is understood that a prolonged absence of information creates frustration, isolation, and gross inefficiencies. While the previous point may go without saying, the problem won't go away without a focused and concerted effort on behalf of the leader and his or her team.

Here are 7 tools and techniques to strengthen your communication strategy and enhance your communication effectiveness.

Be Intentional. Becoming a more effective communicator starts with becoming intentional, thoughtful, and strategic. Every message has a purpose, and every message adds to the perception of your effectiveness, or it adds to the perception of your ineffectiveness as a leader.

Rebuke The Curse. It is easy to mistakenly assume that because you are so intimately acquainted with the data, that your direct reports are equally as acquainted - this is usually not the case. This mistake is commonly referred to as the curse of knowledge. Break the curse by acknowledging not everyone has the same level of awareness and familiarity with the data. Strive to share to your employee's level of understanding, but don't get trapped by the assumption that they already know all of what you know.

"As of Right Now," Business situations are always in flux. Remind your employees that the current update is based on what you know at the moment, and as conditions and circumstances change a new update will be made.

Get Comfortable With Repetition. There is no such thing as a one and done message in the workplace. Get comfortable with saying the same thing, sometimes in exactly the same way, if you expect to have your message heard and understood.

Provide Context. A great communicator doesn't leave the interpretation of his or her message to chance. Don't just provide the update, but also make sure you help the employees appreciate the news and its nuances. They want to know what impact the update has on them and the work they do.

Utilize Multiple Channels. Today, leaders have a variety of channels of communication at their disposal. The list includes:

Bulletin Boards	Calendars	Closed Circuit	Hot News	Texting
Intranet	Project Meetings	Town Hall	Social Media	Face-to-Face

Be sure to avail yourself of the full gamut, and resist the temptation to rely on a restricted few.

Recruit Messengers. Employees can grow tone-deaf after hearing from the same messenger. Consider enlisting team leaders, shift supervisors, and employees of influence in reiterating the key points of your message. Not only will you regain the attention of the team, but you can also increase the comprehension and retention of the message.

These 7 tools and techniques represent immediate remedies to address the challenges of poor communication between leaders and direct reports - of equal importance, to reduce the reoccurrence of these challenges.

The repeated asking of the question "What's goin' on?" is a tell-tale sign of communications problems, with potentially devastating consequences. Without effective communication, no leader can hope to leverage the entrusted human capital in a responsible and profitable manner.

Soulful Leadership Lesson: If your team members are asking, "What's goin' on?" for any reason other than an informal greeting; their asking may be indicative of communication problems. Leaders, who struggle to keep employees apprised of the current state of affairs and potential next steps, will struggle even more so to be respected and effective in their roles. The lesson is simple; great communication translates to an incredible competitive advantage.

Ain't No Mountain High Enough

How To Overcome The 3 Unavoidable Obstacles To Teamwork

"Teamwork is an exotic expedition, and equally as demanding. The trek is arduous, but the results are astonishing."

When discussing the topic of teamwork, the National Aeronautics and Space Administration (NASA) immediately comes to mind. Working in a realm that many outsiders regard only as "science fiction," this organization has helped us to boldly go where no one has ever gone before. Their accomplishments include the Apollo Moon Landing, Skylab space station, and the Space Shuttle, just to name a few. None of these mind-blowing accomplishments was possible without teamwork.

Virtually no one works totally alone! We have many coworkers, colleagues, and collaborators who contribute either directly or indirectly to our successes. That being the case, we all rely on teamwork to reach our goals.

Of course, the trek to reach those goals is dotted with many difficulties, dangers, and disappointments. Every (wise) leader knows the team needs to find their truest and purest motivation if they are to endure those inevitable episodes of hardship. That (wise) leader also knows that team members must affirm and reaffirm their commitment to the mission and to each other throughout the trek. That is a very tall order to fill. Where can you find assistance? Perhaps there are poignant and relevant lessons to glean from unusual and unlikely sources, say… a Motown hit?

If you had to name a Motown chart-topper, a number one hit, which embodies the essence of teamwork and commitment, which song would it be for you?

Hands down, if there were an unofficial theme song for teamwork (and all the challenging nuances), "Ain't No Mountain High Enough" would have to be that song. It is perfect. The fact that the song was written as a collaboration of Ashford and Simpson, and that Tammi Terrell and Marvin Gaye performed the original recording as a duet validates that the spirit of the song aligns with the ideals of commitment and teamwork. So, all of those reasons, coupled with the song's universal appeal, substantiates its suitability as Motown's teamwork anthem.

Teamwork is tough work. It becomes even tougher if team members lack the right attitude and the proper level of commitment. Cultivating the right attitude and proper commitment is anything but a once and done endeavor. You, as the leader, must help the team to believe in the vision and the mission. Additionally, you must help the team to believe in each other. And yes, you will have to encourage them to persevere. With those goals in mind, you can look to the chorus of Motown's teamwork anthem for inspiration, insight, and instruction.

In the chorus, there are three landforms presented. Each can represent either an impediment to or an implement of team greatness. As you continue to grow as a leader, you will become intimately acquainted with each of these pivotal elements. Let's take a closer look at each landform as it pertains to teamwork and team dynamics.

Landform #1 - The Mountain - *"Ain't no mountain high enough."* Every team has its Mount Everest.

In teamwork, the mountain represents the significance and magnitude of what the team seeks to achieve. Fact: The more audacious and bodacious the goal, the higher the mountain.

Big goals require the leader to have big faith and unwavering confidence in the skillsets of the team. These two components must exist, and be convincingly communicated before the team seriously considers the undertaking. If the team senses the leader is questioning the probability of achieving the goal, the trek will be doubly difficult. Quite often, if the person who holds the title of "leader" lacks this faith and confidence, there will emerge from the group another individual who will become a de facto leader. After all, who wants to follow a leader who is expecting you to fail?

The leader must keep the team motivated and moving onward and upward toward the peak. This requires continual reminders of the mission and vision, of the big picture, and reminding the team of the full gamut of constituents poised to benefit from the accomplishment. It also requires that the leader recurrently remind the team that even though the goal is presently out of their grasp, it is surely not out of their reach.

In the celebrated words of the world-class mountaineer, George Mallory, when asked why he wanted to climb Mount Everest, he replied, "Because it's there." For Mallory, that was motivation enough, but each team member must tap into his or her individual "why" for scaling the mountain. Some of the reasons may be intensely personal, while others may be profoundly philosophical; the point is they must have and know their "why." Each team member has to believe, as he or she stands in the shadows of towering peaks, that collectively, the team can scale its Mount Everest.

Landform #2 - The Valley – *"Ain't no valley low enough."* It is called Death Valley for a reason.

Occasionally, someone attempts something for the very first time, and he or she becomes an instant success. However, that isn't the world that most of us live in, and that isn't the experience for most work teams either. In the real world, you have to face a few valleys as you move from one success to the next. As a leader, you have to be prepared to contend with the valley floor experiences if you think you are ever going to have any mountaintop experiences.

By its very definition, a valley suggests depression. Team members will become disillusioned for many reasons; one key contributor to their disillusionment is a mounting cache of failures. To combat this, you must reiterate that failures (negative outcomes) are a part of the discovery and growth process. It is particularly helpful if the leader adeptly frames and reframes the negative outcome as a gift, more specifically, as a learning opportunity.

In an odd and counterintuitive way, each failure brings your team closer to the mountain peak. The ironic truth is that the grander the goal, the more opportunities you have for negative outcomes. Imagine stacking each failure one on top of the other; eventually, the stack will breach the threshold of your breakthrough. Einstein and Latimer learned and utilized this approach during their experimentation to create the perfect light bulb filament. What if they had given up after producing their first negative outcome?

The valley of disappointment and discouragement can be a very low spot for the team. That is true. However, the key to survival and success is to ensure they don't take up residence in the valley.

Landform #3 - The River – *"Ain't no river wide enough."* May the powerful torrents of distraction be no match for your unfaltering focus.

If you aren't careful, your team can end up feeling as if they are in a perpetual monsoon season. They can feel that every path of progress is suddenly flooded by a raging river of distractions. Each distraction has the potential to sweep the team hopelessly off task. Without a laser focus on the immediate goals and objectives, the team will be swept downstream by distractions such as scope creep, function creep, mission creep, and the ever-present nemesis - second-guessing. A laser beam focus is required to ford the mighty river of distraction if you are to accomplish great things.

There is no doubt that distractions, large and small, have destroyed many projects, organizations, even lives. As the leader, you must seek to minimize both the frequency and duration of distractions within your sphere of influence. This is absolutely essential if you want to experience the greatest ROI on your team's aspirations and contributions.

Here again, the (wise) leader understands that not all distractions are imposed externally. A team's internal dynamics can serve as a monumental distraction to goal accomplishment as well. Teamwork becomes even tougher when team dynamics are strained and dysfunctional. It is vitally important to establish protocols on how the team will deal with these internal distractions, even before a situation arises. It is equally as important to operationalize those protocols by ensuring all team members have the requisite skills to execute what the protocols prescribe.

Humankind has found many creative ways to cross tempestuous rivers around the globe; as a leader, you must be similarly creative to ensure the rivers of distractions are crossed expeditiously and efficiently. Doing so is crucial to creating and delivering world-class results.

Each land formation represents a specific challenge and requires a specific action on behalf of you, the leader:

The Mountain represents the significance and magnitude of the goal.
Share the big picture - it inspires the team.
Explore each team member's personal motivation for achieving the goal.
Stress the significance of each team member's contribution to the goal.

The Valley represents the episodes of disappointment and discouragement.
Remind the team that failure is a part of the discovery process.
Setbacks are merely opportunities to clarify your thinking and refine your approach.
Celebrate small wins – enthusiastically. This helps to abate the sting of disappointment.
If you don't survive the valley floor, there will be no mountaintop experience.

The River represents the torrential floodwaters of distraction.

Establish team protocols for addressing internal and external distractions.

Don't allow tiny tributaries to become torrential rivers of distraction.

Keep the team focused on how the task at hand brings them closer to the goal.

Ensure that team members are skilled at addressing distracting internal dynamics.

Every team is different and has a unique personality. Yet, every team will have to triumph over the three landforms referenced in the chorus of this great anthem.

When your team can sing the lyrics of Tammi and Marvin's classic hit (and truly embrace that passion and commitment), then your team will be positioned to accomplish big and bodacious goals. *"Ain't no mountain high enough"* to stop you!

Soulful Leadership Lesson: Teamwork is tough work. It becomes even tougher if team members lack the right attitude and the proper level of commitment. The unofficial anthem for teamwork, "Ain't No Mountain High Enough," provides key insight into what a leader must prepare the team to encounter and overcome. The **Mountain** represents the significance and magnitude of the goal. The **Valley** represents the episodes of disappointment and discouragement. The **River** represents the torrential floodwaters of distractions. With proper preparation and dynamic leadership, your team will sing the chorus from the heights of their mountain, during the lows of their valley, and on the other side of their rivers.

Smiling Faces Sometimes

How To Promote A Culture Of Trust By Leveraging The T.R.U.S.T. Grid™

"The ability to work in an environment free of distractions, dysfunction, and distrust is not only a reasonable expectation but for many top performers it is a condition of continued employment."

In the highly acclaimed cinematic marvel, 300, the Spartans learned that one of their own, one who had smiled with ambition and admiration, had cowardly betrayed them. The culprit was none other than Ephialtes of Trachis. In a blind fit of revenge after being rejected by Leonidas, Ephialtes revealed to the enemy Persian King, King Xerxes, a secret route by which to launch a surprise attack against the Grecian troops.

Smiles!

Wouldn't it be great to emerge from your office to find your associates cooperating, collaborating, coalescing -- and smiling?

What would their smiles signify? Their smiles might confirm that all is well, and there is absolutely no need for any further examination or exploration. Their smiles could indicate that each employee has abandoned any personal agenda, and instead is opting to embrace the team's agenda. Their smiles could symbolize that for this team, respect, authenticity, and candor are the cornerstone of every interpersonal interaction. Their smiles could indicate that each member of the team trusts all other members - - including you - - the leader, explicitly. Then, there is the possibility that none of that is true.

In Western societies, a smile connotes contentment, friendliness, satisfaction, happiness, and pleasure. Consequently, leaders often interpret smiling faces in the breakroom and smiling faces in the boardroom to be both evidence and measure of openness and trust. Glass half-full thinking at its best? Perhaps. Of course, optimism has its place, but let's not ignore the possibility (probability) that for many employees their smile is nothing more than a requisite accessory to the company uniform. That smile, when contrasted to the employees' experiences, may actually be remarkably misleading.

Any leader looking for sage counsel regarding interpreting smiles and assessing the authenticity of a smile would do well to heed the wisdom of the psychedelic-soul group the Undisputed Truth. Via their 1971 illuminating hit, "Smiling Faces Sometimes," the Undisputed Truth provided truly timeless advice when they taught us "Smiling faces sometimes, they don't tell the truth." That song was then, and is now, nothing short of a leadership (life) coaching session ingenuously presented against a musical backdrop.

While smiles are comforting to most leaders, there is a critically important truth to acknowledge regarding smiling faces in the workplace. The caveat is clear and concise; don't be hoodwinked. *Just because you see smiles, doesn't mean the undercurrents of mistrust and distrust aren't swirling just under the surface. Unhealthy dynamics, lack of commitment, and counterproductive attitudes, concealed just under the surface, eventually result in open dysfunction and devastation.*

The surreptitious assault on trust among coworkers, colleagues, leaders and direct reports is pervasive and unrelenting. This assault shouldn't be underestimated and can't be overstated. The destructive power of unseen forces; those operating under the surface, is exemplified in the process resulting in the creation of an urban sinkhole.

In May of 2014, as a result of a ruptured water main, an urban sinkhole emerged in the middle of a busy Manhattan Boulevard. What appeared to be a calm, pleasant, peaceful, even an ordinary situation, was about to become anything but ordinary. Water from the broken water main quickly eroded the street's substrate. Straightaway, a huge section of thoroughfare collapsed creating a gaping sinkhole. The spectacle left bystanders perplexed and stunned. Metaphorically, every team is subject to a similar fate - if the leader fails to safeguard against the process of trust erosion. You just can't afford to let the smiling faces dissuade you from proactively combatting the threats to trust within your team's dynamic. Don't let the smiling faces fool you.

So what is trust? How do you define and describe trust? No doubt, the construct we refer to as trust is, at best, ethereal and nebulous.

Over the decades of working with leaders and their teams, I have coined a term to characterize several elusive aspects of leadership, of which trust is just one. I call them the "Concrete Intangibles."

These concrete intangibles include attitudes and behaviors fundamental to a leader's success, but their definitions often defy consensus. What makes trust difficult to define is the fact that there are several viable components, and each component can carry greater weight or greater significance with one individual than with the next. This is why some leaders consider "trust" to be a moving target.

By way of definition, I'd ask you to consider trust to be the resulting confidence in the consistent congruence of assertions and actions. When we say we trust someone, we are affirming that we believe there to be no parallax in what he or she has promised to do and what he or she ultimately delivers. The more strongly held this individual belief of congruence, then the more fully trusted is the other party. *As the levels of trust in the relationship escalate, the willingness to engage without reticence or reservation also escalates proportionately.*

Though we speak of trust as a trait or characteristic, I believe we are better served by thinking of trust as an organic entity - an entity that must be cared for, an entity that must be intentionally cultivated, an entity whose survival is made a top priority. Otherwise, we are left thinking of trust as a state of affairs that somehow happens on its own, magically. Of course, nothing could be farther from the truth. When trust is a priority, teams and organizations thrive. When the converse is true, when trust isn't a priority, every meaningful business metric shows the impact. The current dearth of trust in the workplace not only suggests leaders are neglecting the cultivation and maintenance of a culture of trust, but recent data testifies to the fact that the current state is one of crisis.

Surveys reveal that levels of trust have been progressively declining in general society as a whole for some time. As such, it would stand to reason that the workplace wouldn't be immune to a similar degree of decline. DDB Life Style Surveys established that general levels of trust throughout the United States had begun to trend upward after World War II. That trend continued through the better portion of the 1960s. Data from that survey showed that between 1967-1968 trust levels effectually reached their peak. Amazingly, during that specific window of 1967-1968, nearly 6 in 10 respondents concurred with the survey statement "Most people can be trusted." However, trust in the United States has trended downward from that point in time. More recently, in a poll published by the Associated Press, The GfK Group, an international market research organization, explored the identical statement – "Most people can be trusted." They found that only slightly better than 3 in 10 Americans agreed with the statement. Such a decline surely has an impact on interactions in and outside of the workplace.

Regarding trust in the workplace, the American Psychological Association found that roughly, 1 in 4 adults did not trust their employers and only about half believe their employer is open and upfront with them. As a leader, you would have to be naïve to think it acceptable that only about half of your employees believe you to be candid and forthcoming.

Other experts in the area of employee trust and its consequences are also sounding warnings. Experts such as Ilene Gochman, PH.D., national practice leader for organization measurement at Watson Wyatt, warns, "Employee trust levels and corporate performance are closely linked." Gochman went on to point out the findings of a survey which revealed that the rate of three-year total returns to shareholders was almost three times higher at companies with high trust levels than at companies with low trust levels. Clearly, trust pays dividends. With data like this readily available, it would be irresponsible of a leader simply to assume that where there are smiles, there is also trust. Such a miscalculation may be extremely costly.

How would you rate the current level of trust among your colleagues, peers, and direct reports?

There is perhaps no one element of the work relationship as grossly overestimated (particularly by leaders), as is the presumed level of trust. I should note that this overestimation isn't without measurable and undesirable consequences.

Low trust is costly. Low trust takes both an emotional toll on the parties concerned and a financial toll on the bottom line. In an oft-cited report, Watson Wyatt established that high-trust companies outperform low-trust companies by nearly 300%. The Annual Edelman Trust Barometer pointed out, "Just as trust benefits companies, mistrust or loss of trust has costs. At least 64% of opinion leaders in every country surveyed said they had refused to buy the products or services of a company they did not trust." Reports such as these should serve as a clarion call to leaders.

As a leader, you cannot afford to continue to merely hope that the trust level is high; you must intentionally facilitate and cultivate higher levels of trust within your sphere of influence. This must be intentional. A laissez-faire approach to trust is a sure first step toward being blindsided by the unpleasant and costly consequences of low trust. If the business mantra, "Time is money" is accurate, then it is important to note that low trust slows the rapidity with which teams communicate and collaborate.

It is baffling that nearly every leader wants to be trusted, but so very few are comfortable explicitly exploring what is working to promote trust in their work relationships, and what isn't. This unvarnished exploration is a practice in which many leaders stumble and falter, but a practice in which immediate and dramatic improvement must occur.

Is creating a culture of trust important to you? Is it important enough to push you out of your comfort zone? Rest assured; this is not an issue that gets better with time. Proactivity is crucial. If you are willing to take a step out of your comfort zone, you will find yourself in the learning zone. Specifically, centered in a zone where you can learn what trust means, looks like, and feels like for those in your sphere of influence. To enter that magical zone, you must catalyze both a new way of thinking and a new type of dialogue.

The T.R.U.S.T. Grid™ is a tool to help leaders focus on improving the levels of trust among team members and making the promotion of a culture of trust a team norm.

T - Truth - Tell The Truth. Trust built upon anything other than the truth is hardly trust at all. When truth is lacking, the resulting condition might best be described as deception or manipulation, but cannot be called trust. To promote a culture of trust, the leader must engage in the sometimes uncomfortable, but honorable, practice of speaking truth. This means those within your sphere of influence should have a clear understanding of how their performance stacks up against the expectation of the role. Those direct reports should also know if there are bona fide deleterious habits or conduct preventing them from serious consideration for advancement or stretch opportunities. The practice of eschewing the truth only makes the inevitable confrontation that more difficult. The wisdom of the ancient sacred script on this topic is most apropos, "You shall know the truth, and the truth shall make you free."

R - Respect - Make Respect An Imperative. To categorize respect as an imperative is in no way hyperbole. In reality, respect is an uber-imperative, and as such, should be a non-negotiable priority. It is extremely difficult to promote trust in an environment cloaked in a thick cloud of disrespect. In fact, disrespect is an active and incessant counter-agent to the creation and maintenance of a culture of trust. Trust and disrespect cannot cohabitate. You would be extremely hard-pressed to name an individual who has been persistently disrespectful to you or to others with whom you are close, but yet you regard that individual as trustworthy. That would be a tremendously short list of names if a list at all. Life has taught us that if I can't trust you to be respectful, I can't trust you with much of anything else. Don't make the mistake of thinking you can enhance the level of trust among your team in absence of addressing hurts and concerns created by acts of disrespect.

U - Understanding - Seek To Understand What Trust Means To Them. You must make an intentional and concerted effort to get the employees to discuss trust from their perspective. These conversations should explore three areas: 1) What trust means to them; 2) What it means to be trusting and trustworthy; 3) Their assessment of the current levels of both among all parties. As the leader, you must explore their experiences to fully appreciate the challenges they are confronting within the team dynamic. It is important to build a consensus on what is meant when the term trust is used within your team.

S - Solicit - Solicit Examples. It is so easy to assume you are promoting trust (or at the least not damaging it) via your current style and approach to interacting with others. Unfortunately, that may not be the case. It is far more effective to seek unfiltered feedback focused specifically on trust than to assume that the trust components are intact. Ask for specific scenarios in which the individual felt trusted and untrusted. Explore the interpretation of behaviors and the imputation of meanings. Ask the direct report to share behaviors he or she uses to evaluate how trusting you are of him or her, and to what degree he or she finds you to be trustworthy. This is a vital requirement in order to move the conversation from theory to practical application. By soliciting their perspectives, you are positioned and empowered to enhance the levels of trust all around.

T - Test - You Must Take/Pass Their Test. Ultimately, trust comes down to passing a test. Explicitly, it requires that you pass the test your direct reports, colleagues, and peers are employing to evaluate if you are trusting and trustworthy. What makes this so daunting is the fact that the test can vary dramatically from one person to the next. To further complicate an already complicated process, is the fact that the testing is not a single occurrence event, it is an ongoing evaluation. Each day via every interaction, you are either moving your trust rating higher or lower. The bad news is most leaders haven't prepared for these tests. Many leaders think they can just wing it and placate others with trite clichés and superficial gestures. That is a sad miscalculation, indeed. If you really want to pass their trust test, spend time in "study group" interaction discussing trust with your direct reports. If you do, it's like getting an answer key for the test.

Creating and maintaining a culture of trust demands that leaders intentionally and consistently engage in practices that promote trust and hold their teams accountable to do the same. For a leader wanting to be proactive in building a culture of trust, the

T.R.U.S.T. Grid™ is an invaluable tool. To increase the effectiveness of the tool, share it with your direct reports, colleagues, and peers so they can give thought to their needs and participate more fully and honestly in the process.

Because trust can be so fragile, a leader must never assume that because there are smiles in the breakroom and the boardroom that trust abounds. Take to heart the timeless wisdom of the Undisputed Truth: Smiling faces sometimes, they don't tell the truth.

Soulful Leadership Lesson: Smiling faces can be a beautiful sight, yet they can be terribly misleading. Leaders should be particularly careful of assuming because their direct reports are smiling, that everything is well. The underpinnings of trust can be eroding even as team members continue to smile. Leaders have to get behind the smile, explore and assess the team dynamic to ensure the smiles are authentic and not merely masks.

Upside Down (Inside Out)

Understanding The 7 Emotional Responses
To Complex, Large-Scale Change

"As a leader, you should never forget that every significant change prompts a series of emotional responses."

The entire board of directors of the Durango, CO, Salvation Army resigned en masse because of concerns regarding proposed changes in how funds are allocated. The board members are asking the community to boycott the Salvation Army due to the proposed changes.

Change! Massive, complex, large-scale change!

When you ponder the ups and downs of the workplace, and there are many, can you identify a situation or circumstance that has a greater impact on the emotions of employees than a momentous monumental change?

Change, whether pledged to be beneficial or perceived to be detrimental, petrifies the souls and vexes the hearts of employees everywhere. In fact, you can argue that there is nothing as upsetting as the incessant and seemingly capricious parade of change initiatives in the workplace today.

Employees are anxious and annoyed. You don't have to search particularly hard to find a conversant eager to lament the upheaval created by poorly led change projects. It's apparent that change creates discomfort and uncertainty. What is even more apparent is that most employees don't like change. More to the point, they don't like the emotional vicissitudes associated with complex, large-scale organizational change. Undoubtedly, that sentiment, so familiar to legions of employees, is aptly captured in the title of Diana Ross' 1980 international mega-hit "Upside Down."

The opening lyrics of Ross' iconic song are particularly descriptive of how employees feel as they persevere through organizational change. When facing involuntary change, the time it takes one individual to find emotional terra firma may be shorter, in some cases, than it is for another. However, the actual process is fairly consistent. As a leader, you should never forget that every significant change prompts a series of emotional responses. Ross' lyrics, in part, read, "I said upside down you're turning me. Around and round, you're turning me. Inside out and round and round. Upside down." My goodness, no wonder there are such strong emotional reactions while moving through the change process.

When you are in leadership, and change is in the air, there are at least three key roles your employees expect you to fulfill. Interestingly enough, the employees won't articulate these expectations explicitly, but if you are negligent in satisfying any one of these needs, you might find your change initiative turned on its head. Those key roles are Architect, Ambassador, and Flight Attendant.

Before we outline the expected roles and their bearing on the success of your change project, let's discuss the emotional component of change. Since complex, large-scale change is a highly emotional and stress-inducing event, it is vitally important to view it through the lens of emotional distress, even emotional trauma. Lest you think I'm overly dramatic, don't underestimate the level of disruption change brings to the (emotional) lives of your employees. There is a reason that idioms such as "Yanked the rug from under me" are used to describe an unexpected or unprecedented event. From your employees' perspective, they may very well feel as if they're off balance and that their world is turning upside down.

One of the most common and possibly most damaging mistakes leaders make is trying to "reason" their employees into accepting the proposed changes. Logic is important, but logic alone is insufficient. The logic approach totally ignores the need to plan for and address the emotional needs of the employees. **While it is true that some of the resistance to change is based on a need for more information, it is also true that a much larger percentage of the resistance is rooted in emotional stress.** As a leader, particularly a leader attempting to facilitate the implementation of a complex, large-scale change initiative you must always remember: You can't satisfy questions of the heart with answers from the head.

Let's look at the pattern of emotional responses that accompanies a change initiative. Surprisingly, the pattern tends to mirror that of an individual experiencing the loss of a loved one. For many employees, especially those with significant tenure, the old protocols and processes were comforting. Those employees had utilized the old methodologies for so long that those practices and procedures had become trusted friends. For those employees, the introduction of massive change requiring the alteration or elimination of "the familiar" is tantamount to the unexpected death of an old friend and hurls those employees into a process of mourning.

In 1969, Kübler-Ross introduced a model to chart the emotional stages of dealing with the loss of a loved one. That 5-part model, commonly referred to by the acronym DABDA, provides amazing parallels to the emotional responses experienced during complex, large-scale change within organizations. By interlacing the Kübler-Ross paradigm with my own experiences, observations, and research, I have identified 7 emotional reactions employees experience when confronting what they deem to be calamitous change. The model is titled **S-DAD-CAI**. The steps of the model include:

1. **Shock** – Typically, an employee's first reaction to dramatic change is shock. Employees are stunned and confused by the news. This shock can be elicited by either an official announcement or by the rumor of a possible change.
2. **Denial** – At this step, the employee struggles to remain objective in evaluating the credibility of the announcement and the probability of the change actually occurring. All the while displaying a heavy bias toward disbelief. Statements such as "This can't be happening! They can't be serious?" are common in this step of the adjustment process.
3. **Anger** – As denial wains employees become angry. They question the motives, veracity, and wisdom of those implementing the change. They lament investing so much time and effort in the old way only to have that knowledge

become obsolete. Feelings of having been victimized, betrayed, or unappreciated may lead to displays of resistance. Those resistant behaviors can manifest in the form of passive aggressive actions (concealed) or overt (unconcealed) actions.

4. **Depression** - During this stage, the loss of the old way and the challenge of mastering the new procedures weigh heavy on employees. Employees continually question their "fit" in the new plan. They long for the comfort and status of the "old normal." Energy and passion levels are low. Employees may become withdrawn and dejected.

5. **Compromise** -At this step, the mantra is "I'll try this, but I'm not going to make any promises." Employees appear to want to embrace the new way but often find the changes difficult and uncomfortable. Employees remain emotionally anchored to the old way, but will "think about" giving the new way a try. However, the employees will attempt to substitute the old procedures for the new procedures wherever possible.

6. **Acquiescence** - As they progress to this step, employees follow the new procedures strictly out of the obligation to comply. Because the employees aren't personally invested in the new process, they adhere to the letter of the manual but offer little in the way of constructive interpretation. In fact, at this stage, many employees see themselves as recalcitrant contributors.

7. **Integration** - In this final step, the employees accept the new way as the right or proper way. This step is labeled integration because the employees not only integrate the new procedure into their skill set, but their proficiency in the new protocol becomes a part of their identity and status in the team, and throughout the organization.

Many leaders would anticipate employees to move from step to step of the **S-DAD-CAI** model in a linear fashion, and while generally true, this is not always the case. It is possible to move from one point to another point in a non-sequential manner. These non-sequential moves are often very short-lived and may be in response to supplementary data relating to an earlier change announcement.

The duration of each stage can vary widely from one individual to the next. That fluctuation is primarily influenced by the degree of significance the employee associates with the proposed change. That is why it is so difficult to accurately predict how long a change initiative will take to reach not just the completion of the installation of the software and distribution of the manual, but also achieve the emotional buy-in of the majority of the employees.

The **S-DAD-CAI** model is an excellent tool to anticipate and pinpoint your employees' emotional dispositions during the mayhem of large-scale organizational change. Having an appreciation for the pattern can assist you in achieving your ideal future state in a more respectful, inclusive, and expeditious manner.

Now that you have a better appreciation for what employees are experiencing as they attempt to adjust to the new normal, it is time to examine the unexpressed expectations your employees have of – you – as a leader in the change process.

As employees move through change they are looking for assurances and comforting; they are looking for stability and hope. These needs are satisfied in small part by their interactions among themselves, but they need and expect the leader to be both intentional and consistent in addressing these needs as well. If you distill and sort those needs and expectations, three roles emerge:

1. **Architect** –Employees expect the leader to design a change initiative that addresses their current needs, and that also anticipates their future needs. An accomplished architect never haphazardly throws a plan together and says let's run with it and see how it comes out. Employees want to know that profound forethought and focus were invested in investigating every reasonable contingency of the proposed change.

2. **Ambassador** – Employees expect the leader to advocate for their needs and welfare from the inception of the discussion until the completion of the process. They need to know that someone is presenting information and insights from the employee perspective, and honestly representing their best interest. Employees want to feel that they are partners in the process instead of having the process happening to them.

3. **Flight Attendant** – Progressing through a change initiative is analogous to taking a flight. As such, your employees need you to look out for their safety and comfort during that flight. Employees need to have preflight and in-flight updates. They need you to help them identify what to look for and explain what they see out their windows. In essence, they need a companion who will support and steady them throughout the journey, and particularly during the turbulent times.

As the adage goes, to be forewarned is to be forearmed. Change is a monumental undertaking, for many obvious reasons. However, there are some not so obvious considerations, which, if planned for and proactively attended can increase the likelihood of your project's success. It should be noted, according to results of the McKinsey Performance Transformation Survey of global multi-industry executives, 70% of complex, large-scale change initiatives fail to meet their stated goals. If the process of change is upsetting in and of itself, just imagine the angst of enduring the change only to fail to create the desired transformation. Can anyone say, "Upside Down you're turning me?"

Here are 3 powerful recommendations to reduce the probability of your complex change initiative turning your employees' worlds upside down.

Don't Plan In Isolation. The perspective of those affected by the change, whether that impact is direct or indirect, should be solicited from the earliest point of the planning process. Plans made in isolation may survive the best-case scenario, but rarely survive the rigors of the real-world's worst-case scenarios.

Use S-DAD-CAI Model. Incorporating the **S-DAD-CAI** in the preliminary discussions with employees is invaluable. It is an excellent way to communicate your commitment to their total wellbeing through the process. Additionally, at regular intervals, you should allow employees to self-identify which step of the model best describes their current state. Doing so can minimize resistance and anxiety.

Master The 3 Unexpressed Roles. Complex change is a collaborative effort. Your employees will need different types of support and assistance, at various stages of the project, as they progress through the change process. There are vital and integral roles for you to fulfill at every step of the way.

Complex change naturally elicits strong emotional responses. These complex, large-scale changes can leave your employees feeling as if their world is turning upside down. To ignore this fact is to jeopardize the success of your change initiative. Your employees' emotional responses can vary at any given point in the process, but your commitment to accommodate and address those emotional concerns must be incontrovertible.

Soulful Leadership Lesson: Change, in some form or fashion, is always present. You are either preparing for a change, in the midst of a change, or just coming out of a change. Complex, large-scale organizational change can turn an employee's (emotional) life upside down. It is incumbent upon you, the leader, to anticipate, accommodate, and allay the emotional concerns of your employees through the process. To ignore the emotional component of change is to jeopardize the success of your change initiative.

How Sweet It Is
(To Be Loved by You)

How To Leverage Employee Appreciation As A Leadership Tool

"Appreciation is a guaranteed antidote for apathy."

"Each Friday afternoon, our entire team comes together to recognize another team member's hard work during that week. We go around the room stating whom we want to "Crush," and also one thing we're grateful for." SnackNation

Appreciation (ə-prē'shē-ā'shən)

- : a feeling of being grateful for something
- : an ability to understand the worth, quality, or importance of something: an ability to appreciate something (source Merriam Webster Dictionary)

"How sweet it is to be loved by you." That is the opening line of a timeless proclamation of appreciation, first released in 1964 by Marvin Gaye, and later covered by James Taylor in 1975. If you know the song, odds are as you read those powerful words the tune popped into your mind.

Can you recall a time when you heard a song and just couldn't get out of your head? Well, **as a leader, one of your primary goals and top priorities is to create an environment so flush with appreciation that your employees find themselves humming, "How sweet it is to be loved by you."** Actually, it should be practically a daily experience.

Without a doubt, employees who feel the love, that is, those who have a sense of being genuinely appreciated by their peers, leaders, and organizations, keep that song in heavy rotation. That particular song, as well as the leadership lessons concealed in its title, easily satisfy the criteria of a timeless classic. It is a message established leaders need to be frequently reminded of, and a message to which emerging leaders must be emphatically introduced. Anyone and everyone in a leadership role, either by title or by default, should become intimately acquainted with the science and payoffs of expressing genuine apperception in the workplace.

Making sense of the practices regarded as employee appreciation, or should I say the absence of such practices, in today's workplace can be a baffling proposition. Clearly, many organizations, and many leaders within those organizations, hold diverse and divergent views on the topic of employee appreciation. Regrettably, in this cacophony of chaos, often the employee's voice is left unsought and unheard. The resulting environment is one in which many employees are left feeling unacknowledged, unappreciated, and fully disengaged.

Why should there be any question as to whether or not appreciation and acknowledgment are indispensable tools of leadership? After all, it only makes sense to express your gratitude to those who so adeptly assist in the actualization of the mission and vision, right? Then why are so many employees left singing the blues and feeling so utterly unapplauded and unappreciated? It would seem that saying "thank you" and "I appreciate you" in some obvious and intentional way should be second nature, right? However, study after study and report after report substantiates that not only is this simple gesture not second nature, but for a significant percentage of leaders, it doesn't even cross their mind. This disinvested approach to leadership is not merely sad; it is also tremendously damaging. As we will see, the absence of clear and consistent expressions of appreciation has a measurable (negative) impact on key business metrics.

When it comes to tackling the rationale behind why so many leaders neglect to express appreciation to their employees, I believe the challenge centers on at least three key variables.

First, many leaders are so swamped by the core (technical) demands of their leadership role that they are struggling to stay current with expected objectives, tasks, and deadlines. Unfortunately, and mistakenly, they see acknowledging employees as only remotely related (and debatably so) to achieving their primary aims.

Second, some of those same leaders, and a good number of others have forgotten the euphoria and the boost to self-esteem that comes as a result of being appreciated and recognized. This is, perhaps, because they aren't being recognized for their results. Of course, the exception being if they were to pull off some mind-boggling success such as an entire market sector takeover, and finding the lost city of Atlantis in the same week. Maybe then they would get a thank you note from their supervisor. But short of such a colossal accomplishment, expressions of appreciation are in short supply.

The third key factor is that there is a constellation of leaders who just don't believe expressing appreciation is necessary. In fact, within this group, it is not uncommon to hear comments such as "What? Are we preschoolers? If you need a gold star for doing your job, then go buy yourself a pack and paste them on your forehead! For Pete's Sake, we're all grown-ups here, not preschoolers!" And while it is true that the analogies and euphemisms may change slightly from individual to individual, it is also true that irrespective of a changed word here or there, the mindset behind the different comments is identical. Specifically, the mindset that expressions of appreciation are unwarranted and inconsequential.

Even if a leader aligns with only one of the three scenarios presented above, and no matter how tentative that alignment, it can still result in employees feeling alienated and unappreciated. Here is a powerful question, might those who perceive the issue of employee appreciation as described, change their minds if they knew the facts? Good question. Who knows? But the more important question is - might you change your mind?

In a recent survey conducted by Globoforce, 39% of respondents indicated that they don't feel appreciated at work. I want to pause right here for a moment to monitor your thinking. If you found yourself thinking, "Ummh, only 39%? That's not too bad at all" you may be underestimating the significance of 39%. So, let me try to put this in context. Under what circumstances would you be okay with a 39% reduction in your compensation? You are working the same number of hours, with the same focus and intensity, except you receive 39% less in your paycheck. And this would be okay with you? Well, I guess so. Because, after all, you were the one thinking

39% wasn't that big of a deal, right? Now consider this, other sources peg the percentage of unappreciated employees at an even much higher level. According to a Gallup poll, 65% of people say they don't feel appreciated at work. Wow! Clearly, whether at 39% or 65%, this problem is much too large to take lightly.

One of the cardinal principles a businessperson learns early on is to invest in appreciating assets and to avoid depreciating assets. What an interesting concept. Interestingly, this principle also has application in leading people. Let's see how.

So let's start with a familiar assertion in the business world: People are our most valuable asset. Of course, we have all heard that phrase many times and you probably have a feeling - one way or another - regarding that statement. Personally, I find the statement to be both interesting and confounding. I'm sure I am not alone. That is because in many organizations, the purported "valuable asset" isn't feeling very valued. The incongruence between the assertion and the expressed reality of so many employees is more than a little striking. Again, the big question is: What is the reality of those you lead, manage, direct or supervise? There really isn't any way to sidestep this truth: if you don't take care of an asset it will soon become a liability.

Expressing appreciation helps your greatest assets (people) to improve and excel in self-esteem, innovation, and productivity, which, by the way, translates to bottom-line value. You might say, appreciation fosters appreciation.

But what happens when people aren't shown the explicit appreciation they need and deserve? Of course, the answer is they become disengaged and often they leave. When good people leave, your competitive position in the marketplace can be dramatically altered. You are left to come to grips with the fact that an individual who was once your ally, now, as a result of their new employment arrangement, has become your marketplace adversary.

Clueless leaders make excuses and attempt to justify why good talent, even top talent, is scampering out the door. Amazingly, these clueless leaders always find a self-affirming reason (excuse) for the painful and costly departures. A popular excuse is that employees are leaving for better-paying jobs. This excuse is often one of the first offered and is ubiquitous in boardroom debates. In fact, research reported by Blackhawk Engagement Solutions revealed that 89% of employers assume that their employees leave for more money. However, Gallup and the Incentive Research Foundation indicate that only 12% of employees actually increase their compensation upon departure. Just let that sink in for a moment. The most popular explanation for voluntary employee turnover applies to only 12% of the occurrences. What about the remaining 88%? For leaders to continue to regurgitate "better pay" as the primary impetus for volunteer turnover is proof that they are either grossly misinformed or incredibly desperate to keep the bright light of scrutiny away from themselves.

Authors Tom Rath and Donald Clifton noted in their book, "How Full Is Your Bucket?" the number-one reason most Americans leave their jobs is that they don't feel appreciated. In fact, 65% of people surveyed by Gallup said they received no recognition for their good work last year." If you are one of those leaders looking for an excuse to justify your exorbitant turnover, maybe you need to come to terms with the fact that in the vast majority of incidences, it really isn't the money that drives the employee's decision to depart. And, for the record, the U.S. Department of Labor Statistics, reports that companies that score in the top 20%

for building a "recognition-rich culture" actually have 31% lower voluntary turnover in contrast to those outside the top 20%.

This dismal and depressing state of affairs would lead you to believe that organizations are woefully inept at, if not indifferent to, recognizing employees and showing appreciation for consistently delivering exceptional results. At least that is how it appears at first glance. So how do we make sense of some of the most perplexing and puzzling data on this point? For instance, in a recent report titled The State of Employee Recognition, Bersin by Deloitte discovered that nearly 75% of organizations have a recognition program. That is absolutely wonderful, however, Bersin also uncovered that only 58% of employees think their organizations have a recognition program. Cleary, it really doesn't do your organization much good to have an employee appreciation and recognition program if more than 40% of the employees aren't even aware it exists. It would appear, at least in many organizations, that the employee appreciation and recognition program is yet another one of those closely guarded corporate secrets.

Those organizations recognized as "Best in Class" by way of employee appreciation, don't keep their appreciation of their employees a secret at all. Their bold commitment to employee appreciation contributed greatly to these world-class organizations landing on the CareerBliss list of Happiest Companies. The latest list includes stalwart names and sector giants such as UnitedHealthCare, Amgen Inc., Novartis, Total Quality Logistics, Metropolitan Life Insurance Company, and Adobe Systems Inc. Leaders in these award-winning organizations understand the power of genuine expressions of appreciation. Albeit, some leaders know it intuitively, while others rely on research results, such as those conveyed by Dr. Paul Marciano, to inform their decisions.

According to Dr. Marciano, author of "Carrots and Sticks Don't Work," for every minute a leader invests in reinforcement behaviors (appreciation and recognition), the employee experiences a 100-minute boost in initiative. Astonishingly, in results reported in the Maritz Motivation Solutions study, researchers found that 85.5% of employees who had experienced meaningfully recognition agreed with the statement: "I feel motivated to go beyond my formal job responsibilities to get the job done." However, 58.3% of those not meaningfully recognized did not agree. Once again, it's strikingly clear that employee appreciation has a bottom-line impact.

The data in support of employee appreciation is overwhelming and highly compelling, but the key question remains, are you committed to modifying your leadership approach to incorporate acts of employee appreciation, and to do so intentionally? You should adopt as a top priority the goal of getting your employees to sing that coveted refrain, "How Sweet It Is To Be Loved By You!" Here are 7 practices to help you excel in effectively communicating your genuine appreciation to and for those in your sphere of influence.

Make Personal Gratitude A Priority. It is much easier to express your appreciation of others after you identify and celebrate what you are grateful for in your own life. Not only does personal gratitude affect your brain chemistry, it can have a direct impact on how you interact with your direct reports. In order to tap into the most authentic expressions of your appreciation for others, start with identifying and focusing on the smallest of things in your life for which you have a high level of appreciation, and watch how much easier it becomes to acknowledge your appreciation of others.

Broadcast Your Intention. Tell one, tell all. It is amazing how sharing your intentions gives others a more accurate lens through which to evaluate your actions. Allow your team members to support you in your growth. So, "broadcast" your plan to be more intentional in expressing your appreciation for others. Simultaneously, make the practice of expressing appreciation a team norm. Help each team member to see that **expressing appreciation is not just good manners, it's good for business.**

Anchor To Organizational Values. Your expression of appreciation takes on import and significance when it is couched in the context of organizational goals and objectives. Many leaders often overlook this point. Remember, the more behaviorally specific and goal-relevant the observation, the more impact it has with the employee. An unanchored accolade is a wasted accolade.

No Strings Attached. It doesn't take long for employees to notice a pattern of being praised just before, if not in conjunction with, requests to take on unpleasant tasks. Such a pattern completely eviscerates the potential benefits of the expression of appreciation. To be most effective, any expression of appreciation must be perceived as coming without any strings attached.

No Respecter Of Person. Not that you need to keep an actual scorecard, but a virtual scorecard might not be a bad idea. When it comes to expressing your appreciation and recognition, no member of your team can be left with the impression that you play "favorites." No one should be left feeling invisible or unappreciated. Ensure you are an equal opportunity distributor of appreciation.

Variety And Versatility Required. There is no one-size-meets-all-needs approach to expressing your appreciation to your employees. Just as nearly everyone can find something they like in the offerings of a smorgasbord, it is your responsibility to serve up a variety of mechanisms by which to deliver your message of appreciation. Versatility and variety in style and approach to expressing appreciation are required to ensure long-term impact.

Become Contagious. As you model and prefect the practice of expressing your appreciation, you will free and empower your direct reports to do the same. To have employees freely express their appreciation one to another has the potential to transform your team dynamic and organizational culture. Never underestimate the power of your example and the power of peer-to-peer recognition.

When embraced and implemented, these 7 practices hold the key to invigorating your team and work environment. As a leader, make expressing genuine appreciation an all-around priority for yourself and your team. You will soon experience what so many researchers affirm to be essential, and for what so many employees longingly aspire – an environment chocked full of genuine appreciation for a job well done. With your unwavering commitment and adherence to these 7 practices, soon you will hear echoing choruses of "How Sweet It Is To Be Loved By You!"

Soulful Leadership Lesson: There is practically no chance of your team every experiencing higher levels of engagement if expressions of appreciation are in short supply. If there is an elixir to counter employee discontent and disengagement, that elixir best consist of 98% genuine appreciation. Expressing appreciation helps your greatest assets (people) to improve and excel in both innovation and productivity, which, by the way, translates to bottom-line value. The classic line "I just want to stop and thank you baby" is a great reminder for leaders to become more intentional and consistent in expressing appreciation to their employees.

I Can't Help Myself

The Power Of Advisory Relationships: Why We Need Coaches, Mentors, And Sponsors

"Insights and instruction shared by an experienced leader can propel you to new levels of performance, reveal new possibilities, and escort you into new opportunities."

Organizations are learning there is a need for specific types of advisory relationships. Sodexo offers three types of mentorship programs. The Bridge program, for new hires. The IMPACT program forms 100 formal partnerships over a year. The third is an informal Peer-to-Peer program.

"I Can't Help Myself" is the title of a 1965 chartbuster hit by the Four Tops. The Four Tops were one of the most successful acts in the history of Motown. They were innovative, enthralling, and unique. It's worth noting that the Four Tops didn't find themselves camping out at the top of the charts solely as a result of their own efforts. They had a team of very talented and insightful individuals who advised and assisted the award-winning quartet in getting from where they were to where they wanted to go.

The truism encapsulated in that title, "I Can't Help Myself," is ageless, irrefutable, and certainly apropos when we consider the challenges of entering your first leadership role, let alone navigating the treacherous and ill-defined pathways to executive level responsibility.

Rather quickly in your career trek, you come to two stark realizations; firstly, leadership development and career planning can be daunting undertakings. Secondly, you realize you need help. We all need help, and that help comes from diverse sources and diverse directions, as it should. The help you need most is always contingent upon where you are in your career and where you want to go. But don't be fooled, no matter how brilliant you may be, you will definitely need help somewhere along the way. Like Alex Haley, author of *Roots*, once commented, "If you see a turtle on a fence post, you know he had some help."

Like many of us, the Four Tops were brilliant, but they weren't experiencing the level of impact and wide-ranging appeal they yearned to create. After nearly a decade of working with great producers, but finding no real success on the charts, the Four Tops were finally introduced to the help they needed. They began working with a team that would take the group to heights higher than even the Tops ever imagined. With the right help, their stars shone brighter than ever before, and the same can be true for you.

Throughout your leadership development journey, you will discover that a great many tools are required to complete your leadership toolkit. Success at the next level is all about identifying and mastering the obligatory skills and developing the expected level of awareness.

Quickly, make a list of the leadership tools you believe are essential to your success at the next level. Take a moment to compile your list. This works best if you write it or type out your list.

What is interesting about this activity is that so many people overlook entirely one indispensable tool. Amazingly, if you ask them to tell a story about how they've been able to reach and thrive at their current level, this "tool" would be prominently showcased in the story, but it rarely shows up on the list of tools. That missing tool is – a vibrant advisory relationship.

When it comes to differentiating various forms of advisory relationships, no one will debate that there is a high level of confusion on the topic. People are confused about the differences between a coach, a mentor, and a sponsor. Consequently, this confusion results in misaligned expectations, unsatisfying experiences, and unproductive investments of time and resources. The information below will aid in bringing clarity regarding the distinctions and the benefits of each type of advisory relationship.

Coach. When you think of coaches, what names come to mind? Most people name coaches of various sports teams. You may have done the same, and that is a great way to begin our conversation about the advisory relationship called coaching.

A coaching relationship can be extremely beneficial in that the coach helps the leader to enhance a particular skill or set of skills. Coaching is a process of fine-tuning how a leader performs or executes a specific task or set of tasks. The emphasis leans heavily toward the tactical.

In the context of business, particularly leadership development, a coach is a trainer. The coach has an eye for what will enhance the mechanics of the client's performance. This doesn't mean the coach would be better at carrying out the entirety of the client's duties and responsibilities than is the client, not at all. No one would conceive of Angelo Dundee defeating Muhammad Ali, Patrick Mouratoglou triumphing over Serena Williams, or Liang Chow outperforming Gabby Douglas. Of course not, however, the coach can help the client achieve a higher level of proficiency by identifying enhancement opportunities and introducing techniques to address the identified deficiency.

Mentor. The role of the mentor and the power of the role is inherent in the coining of the concept. As the story is told, a King was preparing for war and expected a lengthy deployment. The King entrusted the welfare and tutelage of his son, the heir apparent, to a dear and trusted friend named Mentor. Over time, mentoring became the term used to describe the extended process of preparing an individual to step into additional responsibilities. By association, the individual fulfilling the role of philosopher and practitioner was called a Mentor.

In stark contrast to the skills-focus of coaching, mentorship is exceedingly strategic, and at some points even philosophical. As a benefit of the dynamism of the mentoring relationship, the protégé is exposed to a view of the "world" that challenges his or her current perspective. The mentor challenges the protégé to think in ways and from angles that are at first unnatural and uncomfortable. The mentor's goal is to expand the protégé's capacity to think, reflect, analyze, synthesize, interpret, and ultimately, to execute.

A mentor is typically an individual with vast experience and real-life success in conquering the challenges awaiting the protégé. *As a benefit of the mentor's experience, he or she can help the protégé see around the next corner, and anticipate the one thereafter.* These insights are especially helpful when attempting to navigate the politics of a single office or even those of an entire enterprise.

Your advisory relationship with a mentor can provide a 30,000 feet overview to help you avoid many of the presently unforeseen traps and snares. Because mentors are sources of wisdom, counsel, and catalysts of critical thinking, they often become de facto role models.

Sponsor. A sponsor is an active and public supporter who has both the authority and influence to create career-shaping opportunities to advance your career. Because of the sponsor's position and personal power, requests and recommendations often result in choice connections and opportunities.

Because of the sponsor's advocacy, you may benefit from an imputed "mirror halo." A mirror halo occurs when others impute to you a degree of the sponsor's competence. The reasoning flows thusly, "If Meg (sponsor) believes so strongly in Brandi (sponsored party), Meg must see some of her strengths in Brandi. Therefore, I think I do (should) also."

The coach and mentor are invested in the development of the sponsored party, this is true. However, the sponsor's investment is an order of magnitude different. The difference might be thought of as the coach and mentor are playing with house money, but the sponsor is playing straight out his or her own wallet. The sponsor's currency is his or her reputation and credibility. So, when a sponsor advocates for the sponsored party, the sponsor is putting major "skin in the game."

Generally, the sponsor has watched the sponsored party over the course of several projects and assignments, perhaps even a period of years. The sponsor is intimately aware of the sponsored party's previous successes and challenges. This level of "distant intimacy" is vitally important in determining the ideal next developmental opportunity. The sponsor's recommendation must be keenly matched to the skill set of the sponsored party, as failure would be costly for both parties.

These three types of advisory relationships work in concert to prepare and propel you to your next level of contribution in your organization. Undeniably, there may be some overlap in the techniques used in any of the three areas, but their primary intentions are indeed distinct.

There are many leaders, in various roles in the hierarchy, who find themselves needing help in identifying, preparing for, and making their next move. These leaders find themselves rehearsing the identical lyrics lamented and bemoaned by the Four Tops, "I just can't help myself." However, fortunately for you, when it comes to leadership development and actualizing your goal of developing into an even more highly effective leader, there is help available - that help comes in the form of vibrant advisory relationships.

Soulful Leadership Lesson: *Your success at the next level is all about identifying and mastering the obligatory level of skill and developing the expected level of awareness.* Today, leaders, whether new or tenured, moderately successful to wildly successful, all need assistance from time to time. Frankly, we need to hear and heed the words of the classic hit by The Four Tops, "I Just Can't Help Myself." The help you need comes in the form of Coaches, Mentors, and Sponsors.

12

You've Really Got a Hold on Me

**11 Requisites To Creating A
Retention-Centered Culture**

"Make employee retention a priority, or very few of your other priorities will be actualized."

Organizations, such as Mars, Inc., are learning that employee appreciation promotes retention. According to research by Fortune, Mars' turnover is only around 5% in the United States and boast of generational commitment to the organization.

When you hear the name William "Smokey" Robinson, most people don't immediately think - "Employee Retention Guru." At least they don't think that initially. Instead, Smokey Robinson and The Miracles are best known for their dazzling showmanship and their impressive catalog of harmonic rhythm and blues hits. Of course, no one would expect to find sagacious counsel on employee retention in a Motown hit song, would they? No way.

Maybe we'd expect advice on love, heartbreak, or the latest dance craze, sure. But employee retention? Hardly!

As it turns out, somewhere in that voluminous catalog, Mr. Robinson and his Miracles hid a great gem, a wonderful gift, for leaders aspiring to increase their employee retention statistics. That's correct; you can find expert guidance on how to excel at retaining employees from a Motown Hit Master.

Now, for the hardcore Motown fans, you know that Smokey and the Miracles recorded no less than 57 singles, and Smokey has written 20 times that number of songs himself. The good news is that the aforementioned "gem" isn't hopelessly buried within that massive tome of lyrics. So, there is no need for you to lease IBM's Watson to scan, scour, and scrutinize hundreds of thousands of words. The insights and instruction concerning employee retention come directly from the title of The Miracles' 1962 hit – "You've Really Got a Hold on Me."

If you, as a leader, desire to improve your retention statistics, and in doing so improve your organization's bottom line, you would do well to heed Smokey's advice and find out how to really put a hold (retention) on your employees.

"People are our greatest asset!" Surely, you have heard that statement more times than you can count. It just seems that if the statement were true, then more organizations, no, more leaders would start treating their direct reports as if those direct reports really mattered. So, why is it that some organizations are really successful in keeping their employees engaged, enthused, and even effervescent, while other organizations experience turnover rates of epic portion? The difference is that some organizations make employee retention a priority and others are only vaguely acquainted with the concept, to say nothing of implementing strategies to encourage and support employee retention directly.

By way of observation, it would seem that leaders intuitively know that their direct reports are important, but behaviorally these same leaders habitually demonstrate that those direct reports may not be a top priority. Don't miss that; there is a marked difference between being important and being a top priority. Metaphorically, you don't have to think about fuel for your automobile all the time, but it is wise not to wait until your tank is empty before you begin to monitor your fuel level.

You can approach the rationale for investing in a high-retention culture from many angles. Here are three general categories of costs to consider: replacement costs, organizational effectiveness (corporate brain drain), and the depletion of the trust bank. Each category, in and of itself, is compelling enough to warrant paying much closer attention to retention. Yet, when combined, these costs become overwhelmingly compelling. You can't afford to take employee retention issues lightly. To minimize the negative repercussions, you, the leader, must "get a hold on your employees," and retain them!

There are many reasons to invest in retention enhancement practices. This information should be of particular interest to those insensitive to the soft side of leadership and are only concerned about the bottom line. A recent study from the Center for American Progress (CAP) reports that for jobs paying less than $50,000 per year (which represents more than 40% of U.S. jobs), the total cost of replacing an employee averages 20% of the employee's annual salary. Jobs paying less than $30,000 have a slightly lower cost to fill price tag, averaging around 16% of annual salary. CAP also discovered that the total cost of replacing an executive is exponentially higher than replacing other employees. Those costs to replace an executive can be as high as 213% of the executive's salary.

The financial incentives are compelling, but there are other reasons that you must strive to create and promote a retention-centered culture. Another key concern is the impact that high turnover has on organizational effectiveness.

Poor retention rates adversely impact organizational effectiveness. With the continued exodus of skilled and talented employees, the organization loses treasure troves of organizational wisdom and intellectual capital. Exiting employees take with them lessons learned over many years. Exiting employees take with them their insights and reasoned secrets. They take with them the behind the scenes understanding as to why certain processes are laid out in odd or unusual manners. They take with them the techniques for preventing equipment failure, thereby preventing line slowdowns or shutdowns. When good employees leave, you lose more than headcount. Their exodus is nothing short of a corporate brain drain. So while you can fill the vacancy by hiring someone new, it becomes nearly impossible to replace all of that corporate wisdom in short order.

The delta between the new employees' and the previous employees' institutional knowledge, and adeptness in navigating the nuances of interpersonal relationships, radically affects the level of productivity, efficiency, and profitability. This difference exacerbates the cost of losing a highly skilled tenured employee.

A third hidden cost of a low-retention culture is the loss of trust. Employees develop a unique type of trust after years of interaction and intense familiarity. In reality, this type of trust can expedite, enhance, and expand practically every aspect of team interaction. It is also true that trust of this nature can't be readily conjured up overnight. Make no mistake; this is a big deal and has severe bottom-line implications. Just consider the role trust plays in your day-to-day interactions in the workplace.

If colleagues are continuingly cycling through the trust tests with new personnel, they become frustrated, fatigued, and withdrawn. When tenured employees are "unsure" of a newcomer, those tenured employees tend to take longer in opening up. Certainly, they will be cordial and courteous to the newcomer, but they are often far from being helpful on a deeper level. The tenured employees share general instruction, but hold on to those job-specific secrets. With each introduction of a new replacement, this trust and sharing cycle lengthens because the tenured employees aren't sure if the new hire will be around 2-3 years from today or even 2-3 months from today in many cases.

These three areas - cost to replace an employee, the decline in organizational effectiveness, and the retardation of trust building - are each a by-product of low retention, and each an imminent threat to the bottom line. Recognizing this fact, each leader has a responsibility to become proactive in creating a retention-centered culture.

Below are 11 requisites to creating and sustaining a retention-centered culture. Strategically implementing and interlacing these techniques will aid in transforming your organization from a revolving door into a retention magnet. Of course, you can tailor each strategy to fit your industry and your particular enterprise. Perhaps you only need to fine-tune one or two items from the list, or maybe you're starting from scratch, no problem. The goal is to permeate your culture with a system of practices to promote the retention of your most valuable resource - your human capital.

1. **Hire The Right Person.** As obvious as that sounds, it is the key to firming up your retention efforts. However, this process starts long before the interview. To get the proper match of talent to task, you must know what the true and specific success criteria are for the role. Get real clear on what the role requires, and your retention rate will reflect your diligence.

2. **Report To Competent Leadership.** Smart and skilled people are drawn to competence, particularly competent leaders. The basic tenet is that *competence attracts competence, while incompetence pugnaciously repels competence.* If your recruiting strategy includes targeting the "brightest and the best," then your retention strategy had better include ensuring your leaders excel. *Make no mistake; leadership incompetence has far-reaching repercussions.*

3. **"Big Cause" Connection.** Employees want to know and feel that they are a part of something bigger than themselves. They want to know and feel that they are contributing to making the world, their neighborhood, or someone's life better. When they feel that connection, they stay. Reminding your employees of the "Big Cause" can have a big and positive impact on your retention initiative.

4. **Culture Of Respect**. Respect is its own reward. When employees feel, not only that they are respected personally, but also that respect is universally expected in all interactions, shifts begin to occur. Also, when the expectation of respectful interactions extends throughout all levels of the organization, the culture becomes extremely attractive and retentive. *When respect is a core principle, higher retention is a predictable by-product.*

5. **Intellectually Stimulating**. Roles that encourage creative problem solving are very rewarding and are key building blocks of a retention-centered culture. Some roles naturally encompass this aspect more so than others, but every role has some latitude, at least occasionally, to allow employees to figure out a solution instead of being given the answer by a supervisor. A duly stimulated mind goes a long way in influencing an employee's decision to stay instead of deciding to leave.

6. **Overtly Trusted**. The rhetoric surrounding trust is often antithetical to the day-to-day experiences of many employees. Trust must be discussed, defined, and demonstrated - not merely presumed. Employee retention soars in organizational cultures built upon open and trusting relationships. In low-trust environments, leaders learn that high employee retention can be an extremely elusive goal.

7. **Mentoring Relationship**. The quality of workplace relationships directly contributes to success in retaining quality employees. One particularly influential relationship is a relationship with a mentor. Providing employees with the opportunity to see things from a different perspective allows optimism to flourish, and retention statistics reflect that optimism.

8. **Expanding Responsibility**. The brightest and the best employees are always looking for additional ways to grow, develop, and expand their impact. Stagnation stifles their spirits. Affording these employees opportunities to stretch to new levels and in new directions within the organization helps to tick the retention numbers in the desired direction.

9. **Acknowledgment And Appreciation**. Human nature is such that practically everyone desires some level of acknowledgment and appreciation for his or her contributions. Don't make

the mistake of thinking a paycheck is a thank-you note. By recognizing and affirming the value of both the individual and his or her work, the culture becomes more humane and inclusive, which in turn strengthens your retention efforts.

10. **Licensed To Lead.** Employees at every level want to feel empowered to "take action." They want to feel capable and confident in making a decision without fretting over the supervisor second-guessing them. Provide employees with the education and training required, and then give them a license to lead. Leveraging this technique will lead to an improvement in your retention statistics.

11. **Commensurate Compensation**. Wages and salaries have to be perceived as fair and just. While it is true that it is difficult (if not impossible) to buy loyalty, you can, however, subsidize high turnover by paying non-competitive wages. If the employee feels the compensation isn't reflective of his or her skill level and knowledge base, offers from competitors begin to look more and more alluring.

Your consistent and enthusiastic implementation of these 11 requisites will position you and your organization to excel in creating a retention-centered culture. Your persistence in integrating this shift in both attitude and actions is assured of reflecting in your organizational success metrics.

We are all familiar with the expression, "We have to get everyone singing the same song." Well, when it comes to improving your organization's retention statistics, you, as the leader, will need to make sure that song is "You Really Got A Hold On Me."

Soulful Leadership Lesson: Tolerating high rates of employee turnover is tantamount to attempting to heat your home in Fairbanks, Alaska, during the dead of winter, while leaving all the doors and windows wide open. Clearly an inane and futile effort, yet similar are the consequences of low retention. Retention is all about treating people as if they really are your most valuable asset. In order to replace high turnover with high retention, leaders must strive to consciously and consistently satisfy the 11 requisites of creating a retention-centered culture. As you master those strategies, your employees will enthusiastically sing, "You Really Got A Hold On Me."

I Heard It Through The Grapevine

The Organizational Grapevine Is Alive And Well

"Just because it is informal doesn't mean the grapevine is inconsequential."

Intentional, proactive, and preemptive messaging is crucial to organizational health. Bill de Blasio, the mayor of New York City, used a video to address his daughter's drug addiction and her remorse. He opted to get ahead of the negative narrative and elevated the scope of the conversation.

Although you may not have been around in the late '60s (but I'm sure a few of you were), you might, nonetheless, be familiar with Marvin Gaye's super hit, "I Heard It Through The Grapevine." Long before the song was featured as the soundtrack of the California Raisins Advisory Board's ad campaign, it was a bona fide soul classic.

The song tells a story of information passed along via the informal communication network known as the "grapevine." Marvin tells of how he learns, via a third party, that his romantic relationship was in severe jeopardy.

Marvin's personal challenge with the grapevine may not be as dissimilar as you may first think from the challenges faced by today's leaders. As a leader, what's passed along via the grapevine can influence the quality of your working relationships and your reputation within the organization. **The grapevine can enhance or encumber your efforts to create positive and profitable outcomes.** In today's hyper-connected environments, you can't afford to leave that messaging to chance.

Make no mistake; the grapevine is alive and well in most organizations, including yours. I recently delivered a series of leadership development presentations at a Fortune 100 client. Upon concluding the first session, a number of participants informed me that they had already contacted several of their colleagues sharing how beneficial the session had been, their assessment of my skills and knowledge, and encouraged their colleagues to attend. Of course, the participants were able to accomplish this via instant messaging, texting, email, and perhaps other electronic tools, but nonetheless - a modern-day grapevine.

Leaders who have a positive reputation in the organization are in fact the beneficiaries of the grapevine. Their direct reports, peers, and associates are spreading the good news about the leader, and the leader's reputation is harvesting the benefits. Similarly, (in terms of the process, but dramatically different in terms of outcomes) leaders who have varying levels of skill deficiencies - regardless as to whether those deficiencies are technical or people related - become victims of the grapevine. Those ineffective leaders are creating a reputation for themselves that also spreads throughout the organization. Of course, as has been true for millennia is true in this case; bad news seems to travel much faster than good news.

Yes, this is a big deal! As a consumer, how does the reputation of an auto dealership influence your eagerness to do business with them? If a restaurant earns a reputation for poor service or inferior food quality, it would be extremely difficult for that restaurant to remain viable, not to mention profitable. The words of Publilius Syrus, a 1st century B.C. Roman author, have never been more apropos, "A good reputation is more valuable than money."

Let's "pretend" you have a poor reputation as a leader. Now, because of your reputation, you find it very difficult to attract and retain the level of talent your team needs to be competitive. The employees who do stay are reluctant or hesitant to accept your leadership, they're slow to assist in the actualization of the mission, and lack the willingness to forge alliances (incidentally, all of those behaviors are common symptoms of poor leadership). How effective would you be under these circumstances? How would this situation further influence your reputation in the organization? It seems pretty clear, given the circumstances, you are doomed to be grossly ineffective, and your reputation is destined to rot on the vine. That is unless something changes, immediately.

Here are 5 tips to leverage the "grapevine" in marshaling your reputation.

Build On A Solid Foundation. The most effective strategy is to align your reputation with the values of the organizations. You are endeavoring to have your name become synonymous with the core values of the enterprise. To that end, always be mindful of how the message highlights a specific company value. It is worth noting that if an organizational value isn't one that resonates with your personal core values, it will be increasingly difficult to consistently model those behaviors. A values-clarification exercise would be extremely helpful in determining your personal values hierarchy.

Think Like A Marketeer. Every message, communication, and memo, either supports or supplants your reputation. Marketeers know that every message is important in creating and promoting the ideal image. That is why they and you must strive to take advantage of every opportunity. Remain mindful of not just what you want to communicate, but how it helps to reinforce your reputation as a leader.

Learn From The Wild World Of Sports. What is true in sports is also true in the world of business. When teams amass perpetual winning records, winning conference titles, division titles, and world championships – people notice. Of particular interest is the coach who orchestrated the success. In the workplace, a leader who puts together a series of success captures the attention of those at higher levels. Use the grapevine – leverage the grapevine – to herald the "success" of your team.

Use A Mix Of Mediums. Your efforts to leverage the grapevine will be most effective as you use a mix of mediums to spread your message. The wider the mix of mediums, the wider the potential audience. While conversations in the breakroom are fertile opportunities, don't forget about bulletin boards and email.

Be Consistent And Persistent. Crafting a reputation – a positive reputation – takes effort and time. You are deluding yourself if you believe a one-and-done approach will create the desired impact. Negative rumors are like extreme athletes; they can run far, run fast, and run long. Crafting a positive reputation is far more hands on. You must commitment to communicating consistently and persist in your efforts.

Now is the time to become proactive in how you use the grapevine to your advantage. Share with your direct reports the praise they've received from upper levels. Help your team to feel good about their performance and contribution by letting them know they haven't gone unnoticed. In turn, you share with your peers and colleagues how well your team is performing, collaborating, and achieving goals, and shortly, the organizational grapevine will become your personal PR network. I can hear them humming your tune now. Shortly, you'll have a new favorite tune, "I Heard It Through The Grapevine!"

Soulful Leadership Lesson: The informal network is an excellent tool to influence your organizational culture and a stealthy medium by which to bolster your reputation. So, become proactive in seeding the grapevine with intentional messaging. While we can't stop people from talking, we can be strategic by way of what we give them to talk about. In doing so, you influence the tone and content of the informal network.

Hello

9 Guidelines For Creating A World-Class Onboarding Experience

"If the onboarding process is analogous to a 'first impression,' then it is still true that you never get a second chance to make a great first impression."

Onboarding is more than a day-long meeting. At Zappos, the onboarding process lasts four weeks. Additionally, the process is consistent, regardless of function or level. Extraordinarily, after the first month, Zappos will pay "misfits" $2,000 to quit.

Onboarding! A process filled with such promise and optimism, but it often turns out to be the weakest link in the chain when it comes to promoting employee efficiency, effectiveness, and engagement.

You've heard a thousand times the importance of first impressions. In regard to the new hire, your first impression goes far beyond the company logo and the interviewing process. That first impression also includes your organizational onboarding process. It is extremely difficult for an organization, and even more difficult for a leader, to recover from a terribly botched first impression. Your onboarding process is so important that if you mess it up, you are literally throwing new employees overboard. So, what should happen after, "Hello?"

The story surrounding the creation of the 1984, number 1 hit "Hello," by Lionel Richie, highlights the fact that creativity and collaboration can begin long before you get to your new cubical. As the story goes, Lionel Richie greeted a visitor by saying, "Hello, is it me you're looking for?" To which the visitor, Grammy Award-winning producer, James Anthony Carmichael, comes back with, "Finish that song." They were off to a great start. **Leaders must ensure each new hire has the most positive and inspiring onboarding experience possible. That positive experience will reflect very favorably in the business metrics.**

Onboarding is the process of welcoming and acclimating a new employee. Sounds simple, doesn't it? But it isn't easy. There are many misconceptions surrounding onboarding. The first and most erroneous misconception is thinking that orientation and onboarding are synonymous. Don't be mistaken; orientation and onboarding are not the same. Onboarding is far more comprehensive and hands-on than orientation.

Typically, the term onboarding refers to the planned activities occurring during the first 90 days of joining an organization. To be clear, orientation is, in fact, a step in the onboarding process. But, in no way would an orientation, by itself, constitute a complete and effective onboarding experience.

Leaders are looking for ways to accelerate the current process of getting new hires fully integrated into the flow of things. They are looking for reliable and repeatable ways to get new hires to the point of maximum collaboration and contribution as efficiently as possible. There is no question that onboarding is the ideal tool to aid in the achievement of that goal.

However, onboarding must become a philosophy, as well as a set of precise practices. **Your onboarding philosophy must be grounded and rooted in an adamant conviction that the onboarding process is integral to the success of the organization.** That philosophy then fuels the level of commitment necessary to sustain the focus and energy required to create ideal outcomes. You will move far beyond the hit-or-miss approach that is so common in so many organizations, if your onboarding process is well designed, well-tuned, and well understood.

The most effective onboarding process is the result of thoughtful planning and detailed execution by an interdisciplinary team. That team is comprised of representatives from Human Resources, Learning & Development, Managers, Leaders, and Employees. Together, these representatives continually refine the onboarding process. The goal is to consistently position new hires to make their maximum contribution as quickly as possible.

During the first 90 days, the new hire is provided information regarding the legacy and culture of the organization, policy and procedures briefings, tours and introductions. Sound good? Not so much. This is nothing more than the template of a typical orientation. And, if that is all the new hire gets, the odds are that they won't stay long. You must do more. **Acclimation and inculcation take time, significantly more time than a two-hour overview or a two-day orientation.**

Additionally, the new hire needs the leader to share true demands and expectations of the role and revisit the job description translating the duties and responsibilities into actionable tasks. This goes beyond simply presenting the new hire a printed sheet of duties. A skills assessment may be required to tailor the onboarding process to address the specific needs of the new hire. He or she will also need to understand the interconnectedness of the team and all other departments with whom the team interacts. Amid all this activity, the leader must begin cultivating a transparent and trusting relationship with the new hire, and to do so intentionally. The leader and the new hire need to explore expectations they have of the relationship and elaborate on their individual styles of interacting. Ideally, this type of dialogue will become commonplace in the relationship.

As you can see, there is a great deal more to conducting an effective onboarding process than meets the eye. The key word here is process.

Dr. W. Edwards Deming's "85/15 Rule" highlights the importance and power of a system (process). Deming's rule states that the system is responsible for 85% of an employee's effectiveness; the employee only 15%. Because people are a little more complicated and unpredictable than fabricated parts and pieces, the immutability of the 85/15 Rule can be debated. But, what can't be debated is the fact that the quality and thoroughness of the onboarding process has a profound impact on the bottom line.

The glaring need for an effective and reliable onboarding process is clear. Research in this area shows that the new hire is using the first months of employment to evaluate his or her decision to join the organization. According to a study conducted by the Partnership for Public Service, 90% of employees decide whether they will stay with the organization within the first six months of starting a new job. A well-facilitated onboarding covers half of this pivotal decision-making period and can be very influential in the new hire's decision to stay or shop.

Data from the Institute for Research on Labor and Employment at the University of California, Berkley, shows that 50% of new hires don't stay with an organization for more than a year. Yet, the efficacy of an effective onboarding process is borne out in research reported by the Wynhurst Group. Their research indicates that new employees who completed a structured onboarding program were nearly 60% more likely to be with the organization after three years of employment. Those savings are astronomical, and undoubtedly, worthy of your pursuit.

So, what should you do after you say, "Hello," to your new hires? Below are 9 guidelines for creating an onboarding process that yields the results you desire.

Create The Proper Mindset. Leaders set the pace in their spheres of influence. That means your team follows your lead on what is valued and what is seen as a priority. If you stress the ROI of onboarding and do so highlighting how the team benefits from a strong onboarding process, buy-in is substantially higher. ***In reality, onboarding is a team undertaking and requires a high level of teamwork. It must be a group effort.***

Start Before 1ˢᵗ Day On The Job. Don't wait until the new hire shows up on site to initiate the onboarding process. Upon acceptance of the offer, you should commence your onboarding activities. Given the technological tools we have today, a simple welcome to the team video would help to set the tone. Additionally, providing links to content on organizational history, accomplishments, or awards all help to say welcome and to establish an expectation of excellence. You might consider a link to a photo montage of the immediate team members with names and interesting side notes listing their favorite restaurants, music, authors, or movies. All of these tactics help to create a welcoming and inclusive environment.

Have The Workspace Setup And Support People Lined Up. It may not seem like a big deal to you, but it is a really big deal to a new hire. One of the ways you can convey respect for your newly hired employee is to have their workspace configured, clean, and ready for occupancy. For those services or tasks requiring the assistance of support personnel, make the appointment ahead of time. There are few things as anticlimactic as waiting two weeks to get a password, a parking pass, or updates to essential software. Taking care of these concerns ahead of time communicates respect and value.

Pull The Curtain Back. New hires are enamored by the prospect and potential of a new role, and that is great. However, every role has a not-so-glamorous underbelly. You will need to explore the responsibilities of the role and the success criteria in detail. A tool to assist you in this task is a current job audit. A job audit is a breakdown of the key knowledge, skills, and abilities (KSAs) needed to succeed in the role. Share this information with the new hire so he or she can set aim on meeting, if not exceeding, those criteria.

Establish The Tone. These first 90 days can be the "make it or break period" in the new hire/leader work relationship. As a leader, you must consistently remind the new hire that openness and honesty are the norms of the team interaction. However, reminding isn't enough; you must also demonstrate that same openness and honesty in your interactions with the entire team, not just with the new hire. Using words such as trust and transparency during your interactions also helps to plant the right seeds early on.

Provide/Seek Feedback - Early And Often. Most leaders don't want to turn their onboarding process into a parlor game of chance. Yet, if you neglect to provide feedback to or neglect to seek feedback from your new hire, you are simply playing a game of craps. Both formal and informal conversations are key to keeping the new hire on track and getting the necessary input to fine tune the onboarding process. Early and often is the recommendation concerning feedback discussions.

Get Upper Levels To Participate. To have the president of the division or the regional director send an email to the new hire has a "celebrity" impact. A simple note (video) can quell any buyer's remorse the new hire is experiencing as a result of accepting your offer over all those other opportunities he or she turned down. If you have a chance to introduce the new hire to any members of the C-suite, perhaps in the cafeteria, the lobby, or any common area, be sure to do so.

Use "Real-Life" Examples To Reinforce Company Values. Integrity, Accountability, and Pertinacity are big concepts. But what do these values look like behaviorally? And even more important, what are the behaviors in this culture that align with these core values. By sharing stories highlighting how current employees live and demonstrate the company's core values, you enhance the new hire's level of understanding and accelerate the inculcation of those principles.

Get The New Hire Involved. The faster you can get the new hire involved in meaningful work, the higher the probability of long-term retention, higher engagement scores, and a feeling of usefulness. Of course, the new hire is new to the organization, but he or she is not new to the planet. Get them to sit in on product review meetings, task force deliberations, or to listen in on a team conference call. Other strategies might include having the new hire review progress reports or client profiles. The key is to get them involved and to initiate follow-up discussions to explore their observations and concerns.

These guidelines will help direct your onboarding process toward remarkable outcomes. Each guideline has the benefit of not just aiding the new hire but also shaping the organizational culture.

When Lionel Richie said, "Hello, is it me you're looking for," he set in motion a creative process that went on to win the acclaim of the masses and many prestigious awards. When it comes to onboarding your new hires, you also want to set in motion a creative and collaborative process that will win acclaim and awards in the marketplace. It all starts with a proper "Hello."

Soulful Leadership Lesson: Onboarding has to be about more than rules and regulations; it must focus on culture, relationships, trust-building, and engagement. "Hello" may be the start of the conversation, but if you wait until the new hire shows up on location to begin your onboarding process, you are at risk of facilitating a suboptimal experience, and then consequently, losing that talent. The onboarding process must be well-designed, well-tuned, and well-understood with the expressed goal being to inculcate, empower and equip each new hire for significant contribution.

Let's Get It On

The "Must-Knows" And "Must-Dos" Of Obviating Sexual Harassment In Today's Workplace

"To take any position other than zero-tolerance when it comes to sexual harassment is to become an accomplice of the sexual harasser."

As reported in the *New York Times*, Vice Media, a billion-dollar global digital media and broadcasting company, settled four cases of defamation or sexual harassment in recent months. Amazingly, two dozen female employees reported witnessing or experiencing sexual harassment in the workplace.

In 1973, Marvin Gaye had a smash hit entitled, "Let's Get It On." I hardly believe Marvin intended his sensual saga to become the unofficial soundtrack of sexual misconduct in the workplace. Yet, even still today, sexual harassment remains a major hindrance to high performance, high engagement, and high profitability.

Popular culture, of late, makes the serious issue of sexual harassment in the workplace little more than pure comic relief. It seems, as a society, we've fallen a long way from the heated and engrossing debates that encompassed the Anita Hill and Clarence Thomas hearings. Today, we're besieged by the buffoonery of the Sexual Harassment Panda of *South Park*, the double-fisted bottom grabbing of *Boston Legal's* Denny Crane, and the asinine antics of Michael Scott of *The Office*.

Many leaders and associates aren't aware that sexual harassment is a form of sex discrimination. The legal definition of sexual harassment is "unwelcomed verbal, visual, or physical conduct of a sexual nature that is severe or pervasive and affects working conditions or creates a hostile work environment." Additionally, experts in the field divide harassment into two general categories: Quid Pro Quo and Hostile Environment.

Quid Pro Quo, which is Latin for "this for that or something for something else," is a form of sexual harassment that involves an individual leveraging his or her power and influence to demand favors of a sexual nature. In exchange for the sexual favor, the "leader" promises to influence processes and outcomes to benefit the harassed.

The second general category of sexual harassment is known as hostile environment. While Quid Pro Quo tends to be more explicit, hostile environment is often more subtle and more difficult to substantiate. Hostile environment refers to any environment in which individuals are made to feel uncomfortable, offended, or disrespected due to repeated exposure to unwelcomed commentary or conduct of a sexual nature.

Over the years, the media has been chock-full of unbelievable, incomprehensible, and reprehensible stories highlighting the pandemic of sexual harassment. For example, a top female official at Immigration and Customs Enforcement resigned following allegations by several of her subordinates of lewd behavior. *The New York Times* reported that Brooklyn Assemblyman Vito Lopez's alleged sexual harassment habit cost taxpayers at least $103,080.

An example of a baffling high-profile case was the Tailhook Scandal. In 1991, a female naval aviator working as an aide to an admiral traveled to Las Vegas to attend a conference of fellow naval aviation professionals. The official report cites that nearly 90 women were groped or pinched by nearly 100 men in a "ritual" called "the Gauntlet." Because the subsequent complaints weren't taken seriously nor handled appropriately, the then-Secretary of the Navy was relieved of his duty and removed from his post. Stories such as the Navy Tailhook Scandal remind us that the problem is not limited by industry or level of authority.

Recently, Uber has come under great scrutiny regarding sexual harassment throughout its operations. *Bloomberg* reported that at least 215 harassment claims had been filed, many of which were specifically related to sexual harassment. Consequently, dozens of individuals were terminated.

Celebrities are not immune to patterns of misbehavior, poor decision making, or criminal behavior. Roger Ailes, Bill O'Reilly, David Letterman, Harold Reynolds, and Michael Tirico all have been accused of alleged sexual harassment. The sexual harassment problem even reaches the hallowed halls of Congress, the ivy halls of academia, and even the sacred seat of the pulpit. As mentioned earlier, this problem is ubiquitous and precarious.

The recent, practically daily, revelations of sexual misconduct by persons of status has been utterly astonishing. Kevin Spacey, Harvey Weinstein, and Matt Lauer are just a few who have been alleged to have abused their power and position. The #MeToo movement has opened a door that many denied existed, and a door that will not be easily barred.

In 2017, The Equal Employment Opportunity Commission (EEOC) reported that it received 25,605 in the summary category titled sex. Amazingly, that averages out to more than 70 complaints each day – every day. And as stupefying as that number may seem, experts estimate that sexual harassment tends to be severally underreported in most workplaces due to the "burden of proof" and social stigma.

While there is a social price to pay, the impact on an organization's bottom line can be dramatic and significant as well. The average jury award in this type of case stands at $250,000. In 2016, the EEOC, alone, recovered damages pertaining to sexual harassment, with settlements, totaling over $48.4 million. The Gretchen Carlson vs. Roger Ailes lawsuit for sexual harassment resulted in a $20 million settlement.

Louis Harris and Associate (LHA) conducted a research project involving nearly 800 participants. The results revealed that sexual harassment is pervasive, prevalent, and parasitic. In fact, according to LHA, anywhere between 40-70% of women have experienced sexual harassment. Interestingly, according to the EEOC's records, the number of sexual harassment complaints filed by men has more than tripled in recent years. Currently, somewhere along the order of 11% of sexual harassment claims involve men filing against female supervisors.

The Society for Human Resource Management reports that nearly two-thirds of companies offer sexual harassment prevention training programs, while upwards of 95% of companies have a written sexual harassment policy. Nevertheless, the challenges of sexual harassment persist. While policies are important, leaders soon learn that policies don't define culture. Instead, practices define culture.

Title VII makes employers liable to prevent and stop sexual harassment of employees. Under Title VII, covered employers must: (1) take reasonable care to prevent sexual harassment; (2) take reasonable care to promptly correct sexual harassment that has occurred. The work environment must be free of the distractions and dysfunction associated with sexual harassment. This must be taken seriously, and you needn't wait until a problem surfaces to take action. The leader must continually and passionately communicate the organization's policy and his or her personal position condemning all such inappropriate behaviors.

The question is: how can leaders and victims collaborate in creating and maintaining a culture that is intolerant of sexual harassment? Here are the "must-knows" and the "must-dos" of obviating unwelcomed behaviors of a sexual nature in the workplace:

Confront: Instantly and directly confront the perpetrator. Use language that is direct and unequivocal. "That behavior _____ (specify the behavior) is unwelcomed, and it makes me feel extremely uncomfortable. I demand that you stop it immediately." This may be all it takes to correct the undesirable behavior. In most instances, this is often the case.

Document: Begin noting dates, times, locations, and witnesses. The thoroughness and effectiveness of the investigation rely on details and facts. The paper trail is vitally important in establishing patterns of behavior and proof of hostile environments.

Report: Identify the channels and avenues established for reporting problems. Make sure the appropriate persons are aware of your difficulties, and your feelings. Reporting the incident is imperative in ensuring swift and decisive corrective actions are executed. Nothing can be done, and little will change, if you fail to report the misconduct.

Remember: *You have the right to be treated with dignity and respect in the workplace. No one has the right to harass another sexually. You don't have to sit still and "take it."* As you have learned in other aspects of your leadership role, "What you ignore becomes more!"

Soulful Leadership Lesson: Marvin Gaye's hit may be a great way to set the mood for a romantic interlude, but the workplace is not that place. *Creating and maintaining an environment free from the distractions and dysfunction of sexual harassment is not just good business; it's good for business.*

16

Where Did Our Love Go?

5 Sources Of Team Conflict And How To Resolve Them

"Where two or more are gathered together, there will be conflict. No need for you to exacerbate the situation by failing to define roles, boundaries, and grants of authority."

Conflict is rarely without consequences. According to Organizational Psychologist, Dr. Matt Barney, the degree to which top management teams had strong internal and marketplace (interpersonal) networks predicted sales growth. The more conflict in the team, the worse their performance and satisfaction.

"Baby. Baby. Baby. Where did our love go?" This refrain, taken from the first number one hit for Motown's legendary trio The Supremes, echoes throughout hallways, conference rooms, and breakrooms around the globe. Where did our love go? Literally, coworkers and supervisors glare at one another with clenched teeth wondering how it is that they now find themselves utterly awash in acrimony. Where did the love go?

Work relationships that were once effective, amicable, and productive have become caustic and costly. This undeniable corrosion of cooperation, collaboration, and camaraderie leaves the combatants (and observers) thoroughly perplexed. All parties are enveloped in profound disbelief and are eminently consumed by feelings of betrayal. The 'us-them' vibe is palpable; the atmosphere is heavy and thick as if the room were filled with the smoke of burning tires. At this point it is painfully obvious; **If the interpersonal relationships aren't working, not much else works well either.**

The annals of history are filled with examples of conflict, even conflict among family members, that changed the trajectory and outcomes of many business enterprises. Consider the feud between the brothers Dassler. Their ongoing conflict resulted in the creation of Puma and Adidas. Family ties did little to bind Mukesh and Anil Ambani, better known as the world's richest siblings. Their love loss resulted in a long-standing rift and the splitting of their father's business. Billions of dollars were at stake in this sibling rivalry.

Unproductive conflict has tainted the business dealings of the Gucci Family as well as the Koch Family. Conflict is pervasive and at times the acrimony can rage out of control. Let's not forget the tragic sagas of Larry and Roger Troutman, and Marvin Gay, Sr. and Marvin Gaye. Clearly, unproductive conflict is common, and at times the conflict is even tragic.

For the record, conflict--in and of itself--isn't necessarily bad. Oddly enough, creativity and innovation require conflict.

It is the confronting, conflicting, and clashing of the "new" with the "old" that creates progress. Dr. Ichak Adizes, one of the leading experts on improving business performance, said, "Constructive conflict allows the best answer to emerge." So, the challenge isn't "conflict," but instead, the constructive and productive management and resolution of conflict.

The quality of working relationships impacts the accomplishment of tasks and the utilization of resources. Relationships are a vitally important component of an organization's culture and are often the "X" factor in global competitiveness and world-class status. If the work relationships are strained, they in turn place a strain on organizational productivity, efficiency, and effectiveness.

Simply demanding that "Everyone plays nicely in the sandbox" is futile and incredibly frustrating. What the team needs to hear is that differences of opinion, perspectives, and interpretations are welcomed and encouraged. And yet, within that expectation, there must be an understanding that respect for both the differing opinion and its conveyer are paramount. Additionally, each individual must understand that the rules regarding the resolution of conflict within the team, particularly interpersonal conflict, are nonnegotiable.

In reality, conflict is inevitable: There are going to be "situations." The persistence and furtherance of the conflict are also inevitable if actions toward resolution aren't proactively pursued. As the leader of the team, you can minimize the unproductive and derisive type of conflict by ensuring that each team members understands and commits to the following precepts:

Expectations: Making sure everyone knows what is expected of them seems like a page from a leadership 101 textbook. It is, and it is vitally important. When there is an absence of clarity, people tend to fill in the gaps with data that supports their individual agendas. Clarify expectations to promote collaboration and to reduce unhealthy and unproductive conflict.

Responsibilities: Delineating and defining the core components of a role, and how that role relates and complements others, is an important step in minimizing unconstructive conflict in the workplace. As jobs evolve and transform, the leader will need to keep all team members apprised of the new scope and range of responsibilities.

Authority: Just as there are rules to resolve conflicts when synchronizing PDAs, smartphones, and computers, there must be rules to resolve conflicts within teams and departments. While each employee is valuable, the authority of each role is not equal. Mapping out, up front, the hierarchy of authority will help to diminish or deter destructive conflict among team members.

Resources: Clarifying the pool(s) of supplies, information, personnel, and a proposed budget of use will help eliminate these frequent sources of conflict within a team. Duplicate claims to resources result in a reduced focus on the task, reduced levels of trust, and reduced productivity. Lessen the likelihood of misunderstandings and conflict by spelling out the right-of-way regarding project resources.

Accountability: Most team members enjoy helping their fellow team members – occasionally. When the sense that some members aren't carrying their weight begins to pervade the environment, conflict is never far off. Enforcing accountability around the performance of tasks is a guaranteed way to put a damper on potential unhealthy conflict and its undesired side effects.

Inattentiveness to the above-listed elements is often at the root of unproductive conflict in the workplace. Consciously and proactively monitoring these areas will ensure you have a work environment that allows you to continually augment your bottom line results.

While it is true the Supremes were dazed and confused as to how a relationship could deteriorate so dramatically; you don't have to set your team and yourself up for a similar state of bewilderment. Conflict is a part of the process, but also integral to the process is the constructive and productive resolution of that conflict.

The strategies presented here, are most effective when executed proactively. If you don't like to hear your team members singing the Supremes' refrain, then make a commitment to educate and equip your team on the protocols to resolve conflict. As much as you may love the Supremes, you don't want your team singing, "Baby. Baby. Baby. Where did our love go?"

Soulful Leadership Lesson: Where did our love go? Too many team members are singing that tune. Unhealthy and unmanaged conflict erodes the key elements of team productivity. Additionally, ensuring that each team member is up to date regarding your expectations, his or her responsibilities, leases of authority, and the allocation of resources will ensure your team's performance is Supreme.

Shotgun

When Going To Work Becomes A
Matter Of Life Or Death

"The threat of violence in the workplace has become so real that employers would do well to provide quarterly education on how to handle these life-threatening scenarios."

No workplace is immune to violence, and many unsuspecting employers are coming to terms with the unthinkable reality of murder and mayhem. Such was the case at the P.F. Chang Restaurant in Northshore Mall in Peabody, Mass. Elivelton Dias was stabbed to death by a co-worker, in the kitchen of the restaurant.

If you were fortunate enough to see Jr. Walker and the All Stars perform live, or on television shows such as *Hollywood A Go-Go, Bandstand,* or *Soul Train,* then you know the dynamism of their performance. If you haven't seen a clip, check them out. They were indeed gifted musicians and true showmen.

In 1965 when Jr. Walker and the All Stars rocketed to number one with their energetic hit, Shotgun, the world was a very different place than what we find today. Or, is it really that different? Sure technology is different, but it seems that some things are very similar to how they were back in 1965. In 1965, the country was attempting to heal and to distance itself from racial and political divides. The nation wanted to get beyond assassinations and church bombings. And the workplace was the site of bitter contract and labor disputes. Sound familiar? But there is at least one significant difference today in contrast to 1965, beyond just the technological advances. That difference is violence in the workplace.

There is little doubt that the headlines of recent years would literally dumbfound and mortify U.S. citizens of the year 1965. You be the judge, here are a few examples:

- On August 20, 1986, in Edmond, Oklahoma, 14 people are killed in the post office when a part-time letter carrier opened fire. He then turned the gun on himself.
- On November 5, 2009, a mass shooting occurred at Fort Hood, near Killeen, Texas. Astonishingly, a U.S. Army psychiatrist fatally shot 13 people and injured more than 30 others.
- On September 27, 2012, in Minneapolis, Minnesota, gunfire erupted inside Accent Signage Systems. A former employee killed six people and himself.
- On September 27, 2013, in Lake Charles, Louisiana, a pastor was shot and killed during a church service. In front of a gathering of worshipers, an assailant fired three shots from a shotgun into the pulpit killing the pastor as he was preaching.

- On February 25, 2016, in Newton and Hesston, Kansas, three people were killed and fourteen others injured in a series of shootings. Again, an employee opened fire in and around a place of business. This time the tragedy occurred at Excel Industries. The shooter was ultimately shot and killed by a police officer on the scene.
- On February 15, 2019, in Aurora, Illinois, five people were killed, and five police officers were wounded as a recently terminated employee sought revenge – with a firearm.

Today, the office, the warehouse, the call center, even the pulpit, all have become practically as dangerous as the battlefields of war. Hardly a week goes by without a report of a workplace shooting, stabbing, or bomb threat. The problem of workplace violence is real and escalating. In case you weren't aware, presently, homicide is the fourth-leading cause of fatal occupational injuries in the United States!

The United States Department of Labor defines workplace violence as any act or threat of physical violence, harassment, intimidation, or other threatening, disruptive behavior that occurs on the job. Clearly, if allowed to deteriorate, many conflicts escalate out of control. Sadly, this escalation comes at an incredible cost.

According to the Bureau of Labor Statistics Census of Fatal Occupational Injuries (CFOI), of the 4,836 fatal workplace injuries that occurred in the United States in 2015, 417 were workplace homicides. This is simply an astronomical figure and reflects a cultural trend. In light of this trend, it is important to remember that employers who fail to protect their employees may be found liable. The Family Violence Prevention Fund reports that jury awards for inadequate security suits average $1.2 million nationwide and settlements average $600,000.

Would you know what to do if a gunman appeared on your premises? The time to prepare is now. Don't wait until it's too late.

Experts in the field of workplace violence utilize a 3-level model to differentiate between various levels of threats. While the model is an excellent reference tool during training and strategic planning sessions, it is presented as a guideline only. An overview of each level of the model is presented below.

Level One: "Early Warning Signs." At this stage, the potential perpetrator may become intimidating, discourteous, and/or verbally abusive. If so, you should immediately document and report the behavior to your supervisor or an individual in authority.

Level Two: "Escalation of Situation." At level two, the behaviors may become more aggressive and indiscriminate. The potential perpetrator may send threating messages to coworkers or supervisors, express feelings of victimization, verbalize intention to hurt others, engage in theft and sabotage, and become confrontational with customers and others. If so, you should immediately make your safety and security your priority, call law enforcement (if warranted), document and report the behavior to your supervisor or an individual in authority.

Level Three: "Further Escalation Resulting in an Emergency Situation." Level three is a full-out emergency. The potential perpetrator may make suicidal threats, brandishing a weapon, present an apparent and imminent threat of physical harm to others, destroy equipment or property, and/or voice irrational statements. If so, you should immediately call 911, get to a safe and secure place, document and report the behavior to your supervisor or an individual in authority.

Leaders must take every grievance seriously and objectively investigate each complaint thoroughly. The thoroughness of your investigation isn't contingent upon the level of violence involved in the incident. A thorough investigation of a lower level threat may serve to prevent the occurrence of a higher level threat in the future.

The more you research this topic, the more alarming the data becomes. Of course, not every incident of workplace violence ends in homicide. There are many other behaviors that constitute violence in the workplace, but as with so many crimes, a vast number of violent encounters in the workplace go unreported. This fear of reporting a perpetrator continues to help fuel a vicious and untenable cycle. It is time for leaders to become proactive in ensuring the organizational culture is sensitive to these safety concerns. At a minimum, the organization must establish and enforce a zero tolerance policy.

Help your employees assess their risk factors. When it comes to reducing violence in the workplace, knowing what to watch for is a key preventive strategy. Below are other key recommendations by experts in this area.

- Conduct comprehensive background and reference checks during the hiring process.
- Train staff on workplace violence prevention, management, and response.
- Conduct annual threat/vulnerability assessments of your workplace.
- Establish a multi-disciplinary team for responding to threats and reviewing the effectiveness of related policies.

This is an incredibly important issue. Our associates and employees deserve the utmost vigilance regarding workplace violence prevention. Experts agree that proper preparation is an effective deterrent. Perhaps, having an enhanced sense of security will also enhance productivity and profitability.

Jr. Walker and The All Stars gave us a lively and memorable tune in their megahit, Shotgun. But that song should remind every leader that far too often, and for far too many individuals, going to work has become a matter of life and death. On this I am sure we can all agree: The workplace shouldn't be as dangerous as a battlefield.

Soulful Leadership Lesson: Everyone knows a battlefield is a dangerous place. But what about the workplace, is it safe or might it be likened to a battlefield? *Undoubtedly, we all enjoyed Jr. Walker and The All Stars' lively and entertaining performance of their number one hit Shotgun. However, what is never entertaining is a shotgun in the workplace.* Workplace violence is on the rise. Leaders must be proactive in creating an organizational culture that rejects any and all types of violence in the workplace. It is time to protect your All-Stars.

Somebody's Watching Me

Getting Behind The Lies Micromanagers Tell Themselves And Others

"Micromanagers are often tortured souls, who in turn, torment their direct reports and associates."

Micromanagement comes with a big price tag. Some of the most venerated leaders in the world of technology, such as Steve Jobs, Elon Musk, and Jeff Bezos, are notorious for their propensity to micromanage.

Ever get the feeling that someone is watching you? Do you ever feel as if you are under unrelenting surveillance? Well, the sobering truth is that you are being watched - very closely.

In an article published on CrimeFeed.com, experts estimate that surveillance cameras capture us roughly 75 times each day. Routinely, your image is harvested by traffic cameras, security cameras, ATMs, and even by cameras hidden in subways and taxicabs. That is to say nothing of cameras on smartphones, laptops, and smart TVs. Of course, some of this surveillance is for your own protection, but there are other scenarios in which all this attention is not about your protection at all.

Parapsychologists, social psychologists, and just everyday people, all agree that human beings can sense when they are being watched. Apparently, there is a system in the brain dedicated to detecting when someone is looking directly at us, even from a distance. The system is commonly referred to as the "gaze detection" system.

Psychology Today published an interesting article on the topic of gaze detection. The article highlighted the research of social psychologist, Ilan Shrira, of Arkansas Tech University. Shrira provided findings from a number of studies supporting the existence of gaze sensitive brain cells. The studies evidenced that when we are stared at, even from a distance, very specific and exclusive brain cells are stimulated. These amazing gaze sensitive cells only fire when we are under surveillance. Even more amazing is what happens when the observer looks away. Diverting the observer's gaze, by even a few degrees, in any direction, immediately deactivates the gaze sensitive cells and an entirely different set of cells are then stimulated.

Now, if you happen to be an exhibitionist, then a clandestine observer really isn't a big deal. However, for the rest of us, it can be an unnerving experience. What if the stealthy observation occurs at work? What if you have a supervisor who monitors your every step, every turn, and even our every breath? Needless to say, if this type of intrusive monitoring occurs in the workplace, it takes on a totally different level of significance and stress.

There's just no disputing that the creep factor and the agitation quotient exacerbate when the "watcher" is your supervisor. Ugh! But, just so we're clear, I'm not referring to some type of sexual pervert, but I am talking about an individual who has a seemingly perverted need to watch and monitor your every move. Specifically, I'm referring to a leader, manager, or supervisor who seeks to tweak everything, whether it needs to be tweaked or not. You know exactly whom I'm talking about - Mackenzie or Megan or Mahesh - the micromanager.

Any good mental health professional would strongly caution against becoming apprehensive or paranoid about our work environments. Nevertheless, that counsel assumes you are reporting to a mature and emotionally healthy supervisor. Given that so many employees don't have that luxury, their reply to the mental health professional's advice might simply be, "It ain't paranoia if it's true."

Recording artist, Rockwell, released a hit single in 1984 that put a melody to the frustrations and resentments of so many employees. The song is entitled "Somebody's Watching Me." Astonishingly, through just a single statement in its chorus, the song emphatically articulates the sentiment of tens of millions of employees - *I always feel like somebody's watching me*. How symbolic that the line is repeated multiple times throughout the song. Its repetition is emblematic of repeated, excessive, and obstructive meddling by a micromanager.

In 1975, an article in the *Economist* introduced the fodder of a new concept and a new term. That new term was micromanagement. Later in 1976, the verb form - micromanage - appeared in *Aviation Week*. Since that time, the term has taken on ever-heightening degrees of negativity. Today, in most circles, the term is so negative that it is considered a full-blown pejorative. But this is not without good cause. Many leadership experts, such as L. Gregory Jones, senior strategist for leadership education and professor of theology at Duke Divinity School in Durham, North Carolina, consider micromanagement to be nothing short of a pathology.

Professor Jones is not alone on this issue. Corroborating the "pathology" perspective are additional excerpted commentaries compiled by Omics International. Among those observations, experts compare extreme cases of micromanagement to the pathologies behind workplace bullying, narcissistic behaviors, and other addictive dependencies.

I define micromanagement as the excessive interference of a manager, supervisor, or leader in an attempt to control the diminutive aspects of a task or assignment. And while the definition may sound somewhat benign, the impact of micromanagement is anything but. Today, the allegation of micromanagement is a common complaint among employees, and quite a vocal complaint at that. In light of the fact that so many employees, in so many industries, are complaining about micromanagement, we simply can't ignore their obvious concerns nor the equally obvious challenges the issue presents. **Plainly, micromanagement is a pervasive shortcoming and a significant obstacle to organizational productivity and profitability.**

These two conspicuous conditions, the employees' complaints and the leadership behaviors precipitating those complaints, create some very interesting and often counterproductive dynamics in the workplace. In his book, *My Way or the Highway: The Micromanagement Survival Guide*, Harry Chambers shared results of a survey exploring the question of micromanagement. His results were equally revealing of the current state of affairs on the topic, and simultaneously, incriminating of the great majority of leaders. Chambers discovered that 79% of those surveyed acknowledged that they had experienced a micromanaging leader. So, said differently, nearly 4 out of every 5 employees have had to contend with the annoyance and distraction of a micromanager. Peter F. Drucker, the recognized father of modern management, may have been on to something when he said, "So much of what we call management consists in making it difficult for people to work."

There are times when an employee will need additional attention; this is understandable, e.g., a person new to the role, or a person struggling to meet performance standards. However, during those times, there should be a mutual understanding as to why the employee is receiving additional attention. The additional assistance and the transparent communication around the need for the additional attention characterizes a responsible and respectful approach to leadership. Unfortunately, that isn't the type of leadership that has so many employees up in arms. Instead, daily, many employees are dealing with leaders who are the workplace equivalents of helicopter parents.

Micromanagers have a litany of "excuses" (lies they tell themselves) to explain or justify their overbearing and intrusive behaviors. But in the end, they are only excuses. This becomes evident when the leader is challenged as to why the micromanaging approach was adopted over any number of other viable approaches. Reiterating here - alternative approaches that would allow the micromanager to achieve the same outcomes without the collateral damage associated with micromanagement. On the surface, these excuses sound reasonable, rational, and even noble - but they aren't. In reality, the rationale that conceives these excuses spawns behaviors that are counterproductive and disenfranchising. Perhaps you have heard some of these familiar excuses, or even used a variant yourself on occasion. Let's give each excuse a test drive.

"I may micromanage at times, but it is only because…"

- I like to run a tight ship.
- My reputation is on the line.
- I'm so committed to excellence.
- I want to teach them the right way to do things.
- It's a great way to keep the employee motivated.
- I just like to make sure everything is done correctly.
- I've been doing this job for a long time; they don't know what I know.

For all of the bluster and bravado that accompanies these assertions, research just flat out contradicts the presumed logic behind these statements. According to a study found in the *Journal of Experimental Psychology*, people who believe they are being watched perform at a <u>lower</u> level. Don't miss that. Micromanagement actually produces exactly the opposite of the micromanager's desired outcome. Productivity doesn't increase; efficiency doesn't increase, nor does accuracy, so that means profitability doesn't increase under micromanagement either. John Rollwagen, a former chairman and CEO of Cray Research, Inc., observed, "We have always found that people are most productive in small teams with tight budgets, timelines and the freedom to solve their own problems."

Let's face it; no one ever just wakes up one morning and says, "I want to be a micromanager." So, how does it happen? Why does it happen to so many? Moreover, why does the behavior persist for so long? Let's get behind the lies and get at some of the root causes.

Typically, a micromanager is the result of a confluence of several independent factors. Of course, on its own, any one of those factors can prompt certain individuals to micromanage, but the more of these factors that are present, the stronger the propensity and higher the probability to micromanage. Here are seven key factors that contribute to the creation of a micromanager:

1. **Misconception of Leadership**. If you think leadership is simply "being in charge" and telling people what to do, you are setting yourself up for a very rude awakening. *Leadership is a process of solving problems by exploring a synthesis of the best ideas available, and then getting others to implement those solutions.* Often and usually, that means implementing ideas other than your own. *Many micromanagers believe their title or role requires them to dictate instead of facilitate.*

2. **Unmanaged Ego**. If a leader struggles with an overbearing and unmanaged ego, you will usually find that his or her active listening skills are also subpar. This leader's inflated estimation of self-importance results in the leader believing his or her ideas are superior to everyone else's. In fact, ideas and insights from others are consistently interpreted as a threat. This is particularly true if the idea focuses on task or process improvement. For the micromanager, consequently, there is very little interest in hearing what others have to say. Periodically, this leader uses micro-aggressions to put and "keep people in their place." The go-to mantra of the unmanaged ego is, "That was a pretty good try, but I can do it so much better."

3. **Accountability Avoidance**. Accountability conversations can be uncomfortable, but you can't afford to neglect this important responsibility. If your employees aren't receiving timely performance feedback, it is highly unlikely they will

consistently meet or exceed performance expectations. Their subsequent shortcomings actually necessitate even more frequent and more challenging conversations. The leader's avoidance of the accountability conversation actually creates and sustains the conditions used to justify micromanaging behaviors. Thus, a downward spiral is established and the work relationship devolves. In an attempt to circumvent the discomfort, the leader defaults to classic micromanagement behaviors – such as salvaging and saving – which are problematic in and of themselves. Finally, out of self-inflicted frustration, the micromanager exclaims, "Oh, just step aside. I'll do it myself."

4. **Fairly Fresh To The Role**. Each new role will present its own set of challenges. Those who are new to leadership, or are leading a new group of employees, are particularly susceptible to behaving in constricting and controlling ways. Such behaviors often align with what employees consider micromanagement. As a "new" leader, often there is a strong desire to stay on top of everything so as to prove you are ready for and worthy of the expanded responsibilities. This "both hands on" approach results in your employees throwing both hands up in utter exasperation and exhaustion. **When you are new, you might want to consider micro-teambuilding instead of micromanagement.**

5. **Former Exceptional Individual Contributor**. Misconceptions of power and authority, coupled with a "doer" mindset instead of a "coaching" mindset predictably create a strong leaning toward micromanagement. Leadership requires respect, listening, and adaptability. Because exceptional contributors are so well versed in performing, it may be challenging for them to be successful in a leadership role, at least initially. The transition requires moving from doing a task to facilitating

the efforts and results of others. This challenge becomes particularly obvious when the new leader is under considerable stress. Under stress, this leader reverts to his or her comfort zone, which is to "do" the task himself or herself. Another challenge for this leader is allowing the employee to complete the task differently than the leader might. So if the employee doesn't complete the task exactly as the leader would have, unflattering and disheartening critiques are sure to follow.

6. **Aversion To Delegation**. Becoming comfortable with delegation requires a great deal more than meets the eye. Trust and training immediately come to mind. ***If you haven't nurtured a trusting relationship with your employees, delegation becomes a bridge too far.*** Furthermore, if you haven't kept abreast of the strengths and deficiencies of your team, you won't be comfortable giving them added degrees of responsibility and autonomy. In the end, all the responsibility stays on your plate, and your team's development will eventually come to a grinding halt. Delegation is more than making an assignment; it requires the discipline to allow the employee to use his or her creativity and expertise to find the solution - without your impatient intervention or intrusion.

7. **A Continued Legacy Of Bad Habits.** Leaders often reflect their coaches and mentors. If your mentor had bad leadership habits, the odds are that you incorporated a few of those bad habits into your own leadership approach. Many micromanagers were the victims of poor role modeling. The problem is, they don't realize it. Neither do they realize how their continued reliance on micromanagement tactics fuels the very problems they desperately seek to solve. Micromanagement only makes your problems with initiative, engagement, productivity, and profitability that much worse. Sadly, and unwittingly, these leaders are truly perpetuating a legacy of bad habits.

As you can now attest, the list of key factors contributing to the creation of a micromanager is very illuminating and thought-provoking. Over the years, as I have presented various components of the list, participants' first reaction tends to be, "Wow! You nailed it. That is the perfect description of my boss!" To which my response has routinely been, "What would your direct reports say about the list?" As is true of so many leadership developmental challenges, it is often easier to identify a shortcoming in others than it is to see it in ourselves.

The list of key factors serves as both a warning and a measuring stick as you continue to grow in your leadership competence, scope, and impact. If you find yourself repeating one of the lies common to micromanagement, take the time to get behind the lie and find out what is driving your behavior. You already know what your desired outcomes are, so the real focus must be on achieving those outcomes without relying on demoralizing and ineffective micromanagement tactics.

Recording artist, Rockwell, may not have specifically crafted his hit to represent the experiences of employees working for a micromanager, but his song has become an unofficial rallying cry against the practices of micromanagers around the globe. Your employees don't want to be under the eye of a wicked taskmaster. No, instead they want you to "watch" what they can achieve when you give them good training, clear instruction, and the autonomy to make a meaningful contribution to the organization. Under those conditions, your employees won't mind singing along as you and they, together, watch productivity and profits move upward.

Soulful Leadership Lesson: Micromanagement is distracting and demeaning. Don't be fooled by the common lies that promote the need to micromanage competent and conscientious professionals. In fact, research data shows that micromanagement is extremely counterproductive. Micromanagers have a litany of "excuses" (lies they tell themselves) to explain or justify their overbearing and intrusive behaviors. But in the end, they are only excuses. It is true that no one ever just woke up one morning and said, "I want to be a micromanager." It is also true that today should be the day that you abandon your reliance on micromanaging tactics.

Neither One Of Us (Wants To Be The First To Say Goodbye)

If Nothing Changes, Nothing Changes

"If the associate can't or won't meet the performance expectations of the role, it is time to consider reassignment or termination of the employment agreement."

> "I was doing just enough to keep from getting fired, and they were paying me just enough to keep me from quitting." - Les Brown

Relationships are dynamic and demanding, as such they are prone to headaches and heartaches.

Perhaps you've been caught in that private netherworld where a personal relationship had grown stale, stagnate, or sour. You begrudgingly acknowledged that the relationship had long since become anesthetizing instead of invigorating, nothing more than routine, and it hadn't been good for a very long while. So what did you do next? You knew it wasn't working, the other party knew it wasn't working, but what was the right next step?

Given the unpleasantness of the situation, each party contemplated severing the relationship, but neither party initiated the action – at least, not verbally. Yes, the relationship was unsatisfying, that is unquestioned, but there remained a bizarre component of comfortability, even amidst the extreme dissatisfaction. Sound familiar?

There's a well-worn adage, which states, "People will choose a known hell over an unknown heaven." This is often the case. You could blame your sedentariness on a "known hell bias" or something else entirely, but in the interim, no action was taken. It's indisputable; if nothing changes, nothing changes. Consequently, you stayed in a really bad relationship - for a really long time. While this scenario is far too common and easily recognizable in the personal area, make no mistake, it is equally prevalent in the workplace.

In January of 1973, Gladys Knight and the Pips released a then soon-to-be chart topper titled Neither One Of Us. This melodic lamentation became a dirge for those feeling trapped in dead-end relationships. The song's popularity was clearly a function of its relatability. The song tells a story of frustration, disenchantment, and disillusionment. Remarkably, many decades later, the song remains a favorite. Some people argue it was the best of the group's efforts. Nonetheless, it obviously meets the criterion of a timeless masterpiece.

While Gladys and the Pips were singing about a personal relationship, there is little doubt the title applies to numerous workplace relationships as well. In many organizations, large and small, if you listen carefully, you can hear Gladys and the Pips singing in the background as leaders and employees grapple in deciding their next move – to terminate or not, to stay or to go.

Leaders and employees are confused. Neither can clearly discern or harness the forces at play in the scenario. For every good reason to take action, they quickly find a counterpoint believed to be of equal validity. However, from the outside looking in, it is plain to see that they are in a tug-o-war between familiarity and fear.

For the employee, the reluctance to resign is anchored in fear of not finding a comparable position of equal status and compensation. So, while the dissatisfaction with the present situation is great, the fear of stepping into the unknown is even greater. Additionally, the current environment is "comfortable" in that the employee knows how to navigate the landscape. From the employee's perspective, comfortability weighs heavily in their decision to stay or go.

Many leaders procrastinate in making termination decisions due to fear of repercussions. Some leaders dread the reproach of the remaining employees as they question how the leader could fire Jannis or Jaheem knowing s/he had a family to support. Some leaders second guess themselves as to whether they've been patient and fair enough with Mary or Marquis. By entertaining this guilt-ridden debate, the leader simply allows the problematic behaviors (worthy of termination) to persist and permeate the work environment. One thing is for sure; every leader dreads the additional paper that comes with a wrongful termination lawsuit.

Furthermore, leaders may find comfort in the predictability of the problem employee's behaviors. The leader knows that no matter what the communique, Anavi or Arjan will take issue with the message. Predictably, eventually, the underperformer will attempt to stir the pot regarding an increase in compensation for his or her unacceptable performance. And the list of irrational and disruptive behaviors goes on and on. Because this has been the pattern of conduct for quite some time, the leader, though agitated, finds an odd type of comfort in the familiarly of the situation.

In order to break this impasse, the leader must take action. While it is true, neither party wants to be the first to say goodbye; the leader is charged and commissioned to do what is right, and what is best. After all, leaders are expected to and compensated for taking action, and not merely making observations. Here are 5 practices to empower the leader in facilitating a workplace breakup.

Hire Slow, Fire Fast. This is perhaps the biggest key to minimizing the probability of, if not averting, a "Neither-One-Of-Us" type of stand-off in the workplace. Many warm bodies may apply for a job, and they may even be able to fog a mirror, but success in the role usually demands a much more expansive skill set. Invest the time up front to find the best match of talent to task and reap the fruits of your prudence. Remember, hiring too fast usually ends up costing you heaps of cash.

Be Proactive. *Getting on top of poor performance and unacceptable behavior early is crucial. The longer the behavior goes unchallenged, the more difficult it will be to change.* No need to worry about offending or shutting an employee down, if the conduct is unacceptable address it immediately before it becomes a habit. In doing so, you reduce the probability of there being a "next time."

Conduct Frequent Updates. After the initial conversation to alert the employee of your concern, utilize both formal and informal follow-up sessions to assess to what degree the expected progress is occurring. While these sessions should be as encouraging as possible, they shouldn't be void of conversation concerning the consequences of failing to meet the expressed expectations of performance or conduct. This is not the time to have the employee rely on his or her psychic abilities in order to comprehend the gravity of the situation.

Separate The Person From Problem. It is still true today; leaders don't fire people, people fire themselves. It is understandable that you may "like" the employee as a person, but it is not understandable to tolerate misconduct because of a personal relationship. If you have done your due diligence by way of coaching and training, then the employee has to make a decision to improve or not. If the desired improvement is beyond the employee's skillset or willingness, then we are still looking at that employee as a mismatch for the role.

Be Fair, But Don't Be A Fool. Your role doesn't demand that you be heartless in how you handle these situations, but it does demand that you be wise. Compassion and empathy are welcomed in the workplace, but not in lieu of competent and objective decision-making. Prepare yourself to do what must be done once you've arrived at that decision-making juncture. Remember, failure to take action only serves to undermine your effectiveness as a leader.

Just as this deadlock is debilitating and disheartening in a personal relationship, it may be even more devastating in the workplace. When leaders are reluctant to terminate unproductive and uncooperative employees, and employees are reluctant to leave for fear of not finding comparable employment, one thing is sure – productivity and morale are on the skids.

Gladys Knight and the Pips climbed to the top of the charts with their classic hit, Neither One of Us (Wants To Be The First To Say Goodbye), but leaders will find their success metrics falling off the charts if they continue to procrastinate in making the warranted termination decision.

It is time to say goodbye.

Soulful Leadership Lesson: Leaders and employees find themselves embroiled in a tug-o-war. They keep holding on to a relationship that hasn't been edifying or efficacious in a long, long time. True to the story portrayed in the classic hit, Neither One Of Us (Wants To Be The First To Say Goodbye), both leader and employee are locked in a counterproductive stalemate. However, just as Gladys said goodbye at the end of the song, so too must leaders step up and make the warranted termination decision. This is a fact, keeping a bad employee for supposed "good reasons" is really bad for business.

I Want You Back

How To Avoid Getting Re-burned In Rehiring

"Due diligence is required when rehiring an employee to avoid being doubly duped and disappointed."

Kronos, a Massachusetts based workforce management software company, actively recruits former employees (boomerangs) to return to the company. Its website states, "We openly welcome high-performing former employees to rejoin our workforce." More than 200 boomerang employees now work at the company.

The '60s and '70s were trying and exciting times. The music was creative, captivating, and contagious. I vividly recall hearing the sounds of the Jackson 5 playing on practically every radio, every cassette player, and every turntable throughout my neighborhood. Honestly, it seemed as if everyone in the neighborhood knew the lyrics to every Jackson 5 song - that's because everyone did.

In 1969, the Jackson 5 released a marvelous tune that eventually became a number one hit. The song was entitled, "I Want You Back." In fact, "I Want You Back" was so exceptional, it is featured among *Rolling Stone's* list of "The 500 Greatest Songs of All Time."

There's no question the song was extremely popular, yet today, for leaders looking to curtail hiring expenses and problems, the song's title can set off sirens and flashing lights as thoughts of employees-past race to mind. Memories of the "pain in the posterior" created by those problem employees makes the thought of rehiring both unconscionable and nauseating. Interestingly, however, many more organizations are finding reasons to not only sing but to turn up the volume on that classic Jackson 5 hit. In stark contrast to the practices of the past, organizations are welcoming former employees back in droves.

Over the past decade and a half, I've provided leadership development programs for an international investment bank in a wide variety of locations around the world. It wasn't long before I noticed something that struck me as equally odd and thought-provoking. I noticed that several of the participants were rehires to the organization. It was intriguing. I had a similar experience as I consulted with a world-leader in hospitality. In that organization, I again discovered that many of those leaders were former employees who had departed but opted to return. This was surely more than a coincidence. So, why was this occurring? Why were so many former employees interested in returning? Why were these organizations interested in rehiring these individuals? Moreover, what are the inherent risks as each party sings, "I Want You Back."

Why Did They Leave In The First Place

Turnover is real - and many factors contribute to an employee's decision to stay or go. When the health of the organization is in question, many high-performers and high-potentials are among the first to read the writing on the wall. Given their natural bent toward being proactive, instead of waiting to be acted upon, these individuals usually lead the procession of departing (fleeing) associates.

Another challenge contributing to employee departure is the level of dissatisfaction with organizational culture. These concerns include issues of respect, recognition, and reward. When the culture is deemed uncomfortable, unhealthy, or unfair employees will actively seek alternative opportunities. Of course, no one can make anyone stay where he or she chooses not to stay, but there is a litany of leadership practices that can increase retention and employee satisfaction.

The Rehiring Trend

You may not be aware of the magnitude of the rehiring trend. An Accenture study reports that 54% of businesses want to reestablish their headcount to pre-downturn levels. Another recent survey conducted by OI Partners, a human resources consulting firm, identified that about 40% of employers expect to rehire former employees as the economy shows signs of stabilization and then growth. So, with 4 out of 10 organizations announcing their plans to "rehire," we can safely assume others will do the same, even though they haven't yet made formal plans to move in that direction. In short, we can expect a resurgence of rehires.

Often when an employee leaves, the leader feels a sense of betrayal. This situation is sometimes referred to as "getting burned." **When it comes to hiring, no leader likes to be burned, and surely,**

no leader wants to be burned twice by the same employee.
Sadly, many leaders get lazy during the process and are hoping
to expedite getting the rehire aboard. In their haste, they often
fail to conduct the screening and assessment required to ensure
the best fit of talent to task. Their rationale is pretty simple and
straightforward: "This candidate has been here before, so they
know the ropes. We won't have to invest much in retraining, and
they will be back up to speed in no time."

Such faulty reasoning contributes to the high levels of frustration
and may affect the rate of turnover for rehired employees. This
faulty reasoning can also leave organizations open to possible
legal issues, as well as create a public relations nightmare.

Rehiring may seem to be just the low-hanging fruit the leader is looking
for, but don't be blind to the downside of the practice. Wise and
experienced leaders would caution you to think twice before taking
the easy route or a shortcut when it comes to employing a rehire. Here
are 7 areas to explore before you rehire a former employee.

Revisit The Rehiring Policy. This is a great place to start the
exploratory process. Acquainting yourself with the organization's
specific guidelines prescribing the rehiring process will help you
to determine if the candidate is even eligible for rehire.

Run It By Legal. Believe it or not, there can be many "sensitive"
concerns and conditions associated with rehiring a former employee.
Many of these challenges may not be common knowledge to the
leader initiating the rehiring request. Legal will assess the proposal
to ensure the organization suffers no potential loss or exposure.

Scrutinize Candidate's Work Record. How did the candidate
perform during his or her first round of employment? If the candidate

wasn't at least an above average performer, you might want to think twice about bringing "average" to your team roster. In most cases, in order for the equation to work favorably for all parties, long term, an average performer may not be the best rehire decision.

Take The Interview Seriously. This is crucial. The interview should be as professional and thorough as with an unfamiliar candidate. An absence of vigilance during the interview of a rehire prospect can result in a great deal of disillusionment and dysfunction on the job. Despite the candidate's familiarity with the organization, the interview must be genuine and detailed.

Delve Into The Reasons For Departure/Return. The candidate may have unrealistic expectations regarding how different things are now, or his or her ability to "deal" with how the organization conducts business. The interviewer and the candidate should be crystal clear around why the candidate desires to return. Vague or ambiguous responses such as, "I just thought it was time to come back," must be further unpacked and honestly explored. Time spent probing here is time you won't have to spend in a second exit interview.

Thoroughly Evaluate Current Competence. Just because a person used to do a particular type of work, doesn't mean they are currently or completely competent in the task today. Very few roles are static in our demanding and dynamic workplaces. Make sure the candidate's skills have kept pace with the requirements of the role.

No Shortcuts During Orientation. We know that most employee orientations are only marginally effective. The rehire orientation is often less rigorous and less detailed because of the employee's prior relationship. This is a mistake. Settle for nothing less than a complete investment in the orientation, including policy and procedures reviews. Throughness at this juncture reduces the likelihood of the rehire relying on a "that's the way we did it when I was here before" mentality.

Rehires can be a golden gift, but negligence on behalf of the leader to treat the background investigation, interview, and orientation with the professionalism they require can lead to misalignment of expectations, suboptimal performance, and dissatisfaction for all parties.

I want you back must be a mutually agreed upon goal for both the candidate and the organization. To ensure each party is still singing the same song six weeks, and even six months after reestablishing the relationship, take heed to the 7 guidelines provided here. If so, you can expect the entire neighborhood to join in as you and your rehire sing, "I want you back!"

Soulful Leadership Lesson: "Oh Baby, give me one more chance...." Those are lyrics from the Jackson 5's hit, "I Want You Back." As the economy allows, many organizations are expecting to re-establish their headcount, and rehires are poised to play a prominent role in that plan. However, this option is not without risks. Before everyone starts singing along with the Jackson 5, we must carry out due diligence to ensure rehiring is best for both the candidate and the organization. Don't shy away from a candid discussion around the reasons and circumstances of the departure and the interest in returning. If you fail to do so, you and the organization may soon be singing another sad love song.

Don't Leave Me This Way

15 Practices To Immediately Enhance Virtual/Remote Team Effectiveness

"A disengaged leader is the last thing a virtual team needs. Absence may make the heart grow fonder, but it only fuels dysfunction and poor performance when leading a remote team."

A disastrous collaboration of virtual engineering teams from NASA and Lockheed Martin resulted in the loss of the $125 million Mars Climate Orbiter. The colossal failure is attributed to miscommunication and faulty mathematic assumptions. Apparently, one team was using metric calibrations, and the other was not.

The world is a small place, and becoming even smaller.

As the footprint of global enterprise expands, intercontinental organizations are collaborating more frequently and more closely than ever before. **The irony of all of this international** *collaboration is that as the world of business shrinks, the teams conducting the business are increasingly more geospatially dispersed.* In such a scenario, no one can deny that virtual teams are an important and indispensable tool of domestic and multinational coalescence. Neither should anyone deny that leading these teams presents an ever-evolving set of unique challenges.

What has been your experience as a member of a virtual/remote team? How would you compare the remote team experience to being a member of a traditionally structured team? The data and the odds say your experience with the remote structure left a great deal to be desired in both the dynamics of the team and its deliverables. In fact, the experience, in all likelihood, left you wanting to scream for help.

In 1976, songstress, Thelma Houston released her rendition of "Don't Leave Me This Way." The song went on to become a chartbuster and a charmed favorite of the club scene. The song tells the story of a lover longing for attention, not wanting to be forgotten or ignored. Today, the song's title could serve as the collective lamentation of remote teams around the globe. Recent research and surveys show that the majority of virtual team members are not dancing in the streets with unbridled enthusiasm when it comes to their experiences working in a remote team structure.

Before moving on, let's not get tripped up on terminology. A remote team and a virtual team are not necessarily identical entities, though the titles are frequently used interchangeably. The common core in each configuration is that there is a geophysical dispersal of some element of the team. That could be that the leader is physically separate from the team, or that one or more of the team members is located separately from others, or both situations could apply. Another way in which the remote team and the virtual team are similar is in their heavy reliance upon technology to facilitate communication and collaboration.

Of course, these virtual/remote teams are not just for conducting international business. They are very much alive and taking on a more prominent role in intracontinental business, even intra-organizational projects, as well. In some of the largest metropolitan areas, organizations may have several offices speckled around the city. Consequently, the "right people" for a special project are scattered between several locations. However, repeatedly getting everyone to a single location for meetings can be practically impossible. The challenges are many, but at the top of the list are travel time and lost productivity. Honestly, some leaders may find it easier to conduct a video conference (VC) with colleagues in Tokyo, than to get a Houston- or Los Angeles-based project team to convene physically in the same conference room. These and similar obstacles directly contribute to the growing use of the virtual team concept. The increase in usage is evident across a number of diverse industries and in diverse venues.

Working as a part of a decentralized team is no longer a dream of the future - the future is now. As of 2016, Cisco WebEx, a company that provides on-demand collaboration, online meeting, web conferencing and video conferencing applications, asserts to power 20 million meetings per month! Another provider, GoToMeeting, estimates that more than 56 million meetings are conducted annually via their proprietary platforms in the U.S. alone. Of course, there is a multitude of other providers for this type of service, so the actual number of online meetings, each representing a virtual/remote teaming encounter, is nothing short of mindboggling.

Based on data extracted from the Forrester Research's U.S. Telecommuting Forecast, the number of U.S. workers working remotely during a given workweek is estimated at 63 million, or approximately 43% of the total workforce. Even more revealing are the results of a different survey. In a survey of business managers from more than 90 countries, Regus Global Economic Indicator found that 48% of business managers work remotely for at least half of their workweek. Clearly, the virtual team is a modern day reality for employees and leaders at all levels. The trend data suggests that virtual/remote teaming will become more and more prevalent and commonplace in the workplace.

Many leaders think virtual means low maintenance; unfortunately, just the opposite is true. Virtual teams require even more care and feeding than a traditional team. As counterintuitive as it may appear on the surface, the reality is that greater distance demands even greater attention. Moreover, the absence of that care and feeding is sure to manifest in bold and dramatic (negative) ways. Trust me; none of those reactionary, negative behaviors (which are also predictable and avoidable) bolsters the efficiency, effectiveness, or profitability of your organization.

In one of the first studies of its kind, professors Vijay Govindarajan and Anil Gupta researched the overall effectiveness of virtual teams. Astonishingly, the researchers found that 82% of virtual teams fell short of their goals, and 33% rated themselves as largely unsuccessful. Of course, such findings help to fuel skepticism in terms of the effectiveness of remote collaborations. Many naysayers use such data to resist remote teaming. Candidly, perhaps, those findings do warrant some concern. However, given the explosive proliferation of the remote team structure, improved leadership and team effectiveness are essential in order to realize the full potential of cost savings and productivity increases.

When it comes to virtual team performance, the news isn't all bad. As is true with a traditional team, is also true of the virtual team: its success hinges on leadership. BCG and WHU-Otto Beisheim School of Management reported results from their study of 80 global software teams. The results show that well-managed virtual/remote teams can actually outperform traditional "co-located" teams. Again, the emphasis is on the proficiency and proactivity of the leader. *If the leader is equipped and sensitive to the unique dynamics of remote teaming, the virtual/remote team can achieve remarkable success.*

Aon Consulting found that by implementing a virtual/remote team structure, organizations could experience noteworthy improvements in productivity. In fact, some organizations that were a part of the study realized as much as a 43% uptick in employee productivity. Far be it from hyperbole to assert that such results may represent only the tip of the productivity iceberg.

"Prevalent, but not perfected." That is possibly the best way to characterize this new normal we call virtual teaming. The sobering truth is that while this structure holds great promise, its imperfections can result in costly inefficiencies, isolation, and insecurities. Don't get me wrong, I am not suggesting that virtual teaming has no merit, but if you are leading a virtual team, you must be purposefully attentive and diligent to achieve the objectives and goals for which the team was organized.

If Maslow was correct in his hypothesis of human needs, and the importance of satisfying each level, then virtual teamwork, as we have known it, seems especially ill-suited to satisfy the requirements of his hierarchy. Of Maslow's five levels of needs, only the physiological seems not to be a significant concern for virtual team members. However, the other four levels – Security,

Love/Belong, Esteem, and Self-actualization – prove to be the areas in which virtual team members are the most vulnerable and least satisfied.

The research is clear; leading virtual/remote teams is far more demanding than leading in a traditional team structure. Maruyama & Tietze noted in an article published in *Personnel Review*, that more than 50% of teleworkers thought they lost out on both social and professional interaction in the workplace. This data is evidence of deficiencies on two levels of Maslow's hierarchy - Love/Belonging and Esteem.

One of the more striking findings validated an unspoken fear of many virtual and remote team members; that of being out of sight – equals being out of mind. As noted in *Organizational Behavior*, published by McGraw-Hill, teleworking can create career-limiting perceptions. This bias was uncovered in a survey of 1,300 executives from 71 countries. The survey found that the executives didn't consider virtual/remote workers as frequently or as favorably in promotional discussions. This was due, in part, to the lack of physical "visibility" and face-to-face interaction. Consequently, working as a member of a virtual/remote team can present additional hurdles to career development and progression. So, the attitudes uncovered by the survey immediately trigger concerns related to three levels of Maslow's needs hierarchy - the need for security, the need for esteem, and the need to self-actualize.

Working and leading in a virtual/remote team structure requires both the leader and the team members to ask a great many more questions, and to make far fewer assumptions when communicating. Understanding a message involves so much more than merely hearing the words or understanding the language. Misinterpretation of the subtleties can derail collaboration.

Remote teams can be a wonderful cost savings vehicle. However, if the quality of communication and understanding is poor, we then lose the vaunted benefits of virtual teaming. When a task has to be redone due to a lack of clarity, it is extremely expensive and counterproductive. Ultimately, what was gained in convenience via the virtual team structure is squandered due to poor communication and superficial interpersonal connections.

In survey data gathered from nearly 30,000 employees of multinational companies, all of whom were involved in varying levels of virtual teamwork, RW3, LLC, found relationship building and interpretation of nuanced communication were deemed especially difficult. Ninety-four percent of those surveyed reported that the inability to read nonverbal cues was a point of significant frustration. Additionally, 90% of the respondents said they didn't feel the virtual interaction allowed enough time to build a relationship. Regarding the sense of collegiality, 85% said it was missing from their virtual interactions. As you lead your virtual/remote team, be cognizant that your team members need to "connect" with the other members of the team. **Your team must be more than a gathering of strangers. It is always wise to look to enhance the quality of the relationships, even if the team is operating in a remote structure.**

It is much easier now to understand why virtual/remote team members would view the song "Don't Leave Me This Way" as an unofficial anthem. Virtual/remote team members are appealing to their leadership to put into practice measures and approaches to minimize the obstacles associated with a dispersed team structure. And, rightfully so. The solution comes down to how the leader leads.

Here are 15 practices to move your virtual/remote team to new levels of respect, trust, productivity, and profitability:

Develop A Clear And Definitive Charter. The best guarantee of success is to know why the team exists. This means to be clear on why the team was created in the first place and to revisit the charter periodically to refocus the team. Without a clear and definitive charter, it becomes impossible to differentiate between what is truly mission-centric and what is mission creep. If the mission changes, or outgrows the charter, then a new charter is required.

Think Hard About Team Size. The size of the team can further aggravate an already challenging team structure. Because of their structure, virtual/remote teams are predisposed to interpersonal dysfunction. Additionally, if the team is too large, it will be practically impossible to create and maintain the trust, thorough communication, and collegiality required to be an exceptional team. If the team gets too large, team members will quickly become disengaged.

Establish Success Standards And Progress Markers. Be explicitly detailed in presenting what success looks like for this team. Share with them the nonnegotiable indices of timely and targeted progress. It would also be wise to remind the team that how they work together is as important as the product they produce.

Facilitate Accelerated Acquaintance. Provide bios before the team actually convenes. Team building should start as early as possible. With that in mind, compile and disseminate a portfolio of team members' bios. This shouldn't be strictly workplace focused. Encourage the team members to make themselves "human" by sharing interests and hobbies, dream vacation spots, or a favorite character in a classic novel or movie. The goal is to provide a multidimensional overview of the individual. This will lead to more rich and authentic relationships among the team members.

Draft Rules Of Engagement. Working remotely is demanding enough without provoking unhealthy team dynamics. Establish guidelines outlining both the concept and corresponding behaviors related to respect and trust. Consider having each team member contribute to the guidelines, express how the observation offered promotes team success, and why his or her observation is personally important. After gathering their input, have each team member sign a document acknowledging their concurrence and commitment to abide by the guidelines. Accomplishing this at the launch of the process preempts a slew of potential problems later.

Build In Time For Individual Connections. Encourage team members to have one-on-one chats with each other to help build trust and a sense of community. They might exchange questions in advance, and then use those as conversation starters. The goal is to build rapport on a personal level. As the size of the team allows, the goal should be that each member completes a one-on-one conversation with at least 75% of the team within the first 45 days.

Encourage Group Connections. Sadly, virtual/remote teams don't have the luxury of bumping into one another in the café or cantina, so they must formally orchestrate for themselves what happens coincidentally for co-located team members. Schedule slots of time for the team to chill together. Have each team member select something he or she would like to share or present. The sharing could be a piece of poetry, a TEDx clip, or a recipe for an exotic dish. The team member gets to choose what is shared; the magic is in the discussion generated by the sharing.

Demonstrate Time Zone Sensitivity. A familiar and painful thorn in the side of virtual/remote team members, particularly those who reside on the other side of the world, is the consistently inconvenient times at which meetings convene. One of the simplest ways to promote respect and fairness is to keep the world clock in mind to avoid unfairly burdening members of the team in specific geographies. Time zone rotation demonstrates peer-based respect for all members of the team.

Provide Periodic Refreshers. Working in a virtual/remote team affords team members many opportunities to offend one another. Invest in periodic refreshers on digital and cross-cultural communication. Cultural differences are often amplified in a virtual/ remote team structure. Nuance and subtleties are forfeited or greatly diminished in remote communication, and with that comes a greater threat of miscommunication and misunderstandings.

Allow Time For Personal Reconnects. To kick off your project update meetings, allow individuals to share a personal achievement or recent experience. You could also have each person share (team size permitting) something he or she recently learned. Ideally, this sharing should include both personal and professional information.

Leader Regularly Reaches Out. Faithfully check-in with individual team members. To build a relationship with your team members, you need to invest in the relationship. Making an occasional call or sending an email to connect with a team member can pay incredible dividends. To make the contact even more effective, consider asking not just about work-related topics, but personal items the team member has mentioned in previous meetings.

Become A Champion. As you interact with other leaders in your network, intentionally champion the members of your team. Given that your team members are working virtually/remotely, they aren't interacting face-to-face with decision makers very often (if at all), so your team members rely on you to trumpet their amazing skills and accomplishments.

Reward & Recognize Often. Be guilty of thanking them too often, instead of not thanking them enough. Virtual/remote teams have a higher need for recognition and reward to compensate for the limited interactions with the leader and other team members. Remember, the reward and recognition don't have to be extravagant; it simply needs to be genuine.

Keep Them In The Loop. It seems that distance makes virtual/remote teams very susceptible to rumors and misinformation. To combat this phenomenon, the leader has to update the team far more frequently and in more specific detail than when working in a traditional team structure. Doing so, allows the team to channel its energies toward accomplishing the team's critical objectives and goals.

Make Candor & Accountability The Norm. Perhaps second only to building rapport and connectedness among a virtual/remote team is the challenge of getting team members to provide candid and timely feedback to each other. Since team members don't actually see one another in the hallway, it is too easy for them to let problems fester and escalate. The leader must provide the team with the tools to facilitate candid accountability conversations. Then, hold the members accountable to have the necessary conversations. This is a priority.

These 15 practices are instrumental in combating the common challenges, distractions, and dysfunctions associated with a remote team structure. More impressive is the fact that if implemented from the conception of the team, these practices can preempt many of the most daunting obstacles to virtual/remote team performance. At some point in its life cycle, every virtual/remote team would benefit by executing the practices outlined above.

As you continue to lead, the odds suggest either you will lead a team with a remote member, or you will be tasked with leading an entirely virtual team.

Today, remote team structures are integral to business success. However, with this structure, team members may be subject to harsh and counterproductive dynamics. Leaders who choose to lead their virtual teams just as they have led traditional co-located teams will soon discover the fallacy in their decision.

It is your responsibility, as the leader of the virtual/remote team, to anticipate and address those distractions common to that structure. This is what your team members are expecting, demanding, and frankly, what they deserve. Their plea is as intense and heartfelt as that of Thelma Huston. Collectively your team is pleading – "Don't Leave Me This Way."

Soulful Leadership Lesson: Effective leadership is never easy. That is especially true when leading in a remote team structure. The dynamics of virtual/remote teams are different and uniquely demanding. Leaders who choose to lead their virtual teams just as they have led traditional co-located teams will soon discover the fallacy in their decision. The new structure requires a new level of attentiveness and the focused implementation of new principles. If you make that commitment, your success is virtually guaranteed.

CONCLUSION

Well, I decided to throw a party, a uniquely purposed and themed party. Not just any old type of party, no, no. I decided to throw a leadership development party! The goal was to create a safe place where leaders with varying levels of skills could come groove and grow. Using the soulful rhythms of classic Motown as the musical backdrop, I wanted my guests to be inspired to think, see, and act differently as they faced the confounding human challenges of leadership. So, I want to thank you, personally, for attending.

A new perspective, coupled with enhanced understanding, is an inspiring and empowering combination. Oliver Wendell Holmes said, "Once a mind has been stretched by a new idea, it can never return to its original dimensions." That is my hope for you as you complete this leadership development course.

As a leader, you are going to face challenges. Only the terribly irresponsible opt to remain unprepared in the face of those challenges. It is equally as irresponsible and doubly naïve to hope those situations will simply work themselves out. We know that such an approach represents a critically flawed strategy. However, we do also know that everything gets better when the leadership gets better. Clearly, you are on your way toward making both relationships and performance a great deal better within your leadership sphere of influence.

Congratulations on investing in your skill development and the furtherance of your enterprise's success. Now that you have completed the Leadership Soul experience, next comes the hard part – implementation. What you debated, deliberated, and digested throughout these pages provides the rhythms for a new song, your new song – a new song that fully and clearly showcases your full potential as a leader.

As a leader, you have been entrusted with an awesome responsibility and an incredible privilege to marshal the imaginations and initiative of brilliant people. What an honor. You owe it to them to be the best leader you can be, in order to expect the best from them.

Leadership Soul was an invitation to groove and grow. I trust you did a lot of both.

I recommend that you pull up a Motown-themed channel on YouTube, Spotify or Pandora, relax and reflect on your new insights and bask in your newly found levels of competence and confidence.

Indeed, this party was an amazing experience. As promised, a leadership party like no other!

CONCEPT CRATE

7-11 Rule - According to Michael Solomon, Ph.D., Psychologist, Chairman, Marketing Department Graduate School of Business, NYU, people make eleven decisions about a stranger in the first seven seconds of the initial interaction ("The 7/11 Rule").

Accountability - In the context of the day-to-day responsibilities of leadership, accountability is a process by which an individual learns how his or her actions fall short of the expectations or standards held for a task or set of tasks.

Accountability Avoidance - The excuses offered for the procrastination or out-and-out avoidance of a substantive conversation to correct performance or conduct issues.

Cognitive Suiting - How the "supervisor" perceives those in his or her direct report will dictate the leadership approach adopted and practices pursued. Cognitive suiting is an extension of the unconscious bias process. Cognitive suiting sets the tone and tenor of all subsequent interactions.

Concert Intangibles - A term to reference several elusive aspects of leadership. These concrete intangibles include attitudes and behaviors fundamental to a leader's success, but their definitions often defy consensus.

Curse of Knowledge - The unintended practice of communicating with others as if the other party has the depth and breadth of understanding and background equal to that of the speaker.

Exaggerated Anonymity - A leader's propensity to aggressively limit the amount of personal information exchanged or shared between the leader and team members.

Illusory Superiority - Illusory superiority is defined as a cognitive bias resulting in an individual's overestimation of his or her qualities and abilities, relative to others.

Mentor - The term used to describe the extended process of preparing an individual to step into additional responsibilities. By association, the individual fulfilling the role of philosopher and practitioner is called a Mentor.

Micromanagement - The excessive interference of a manager, supervisor, or leader in an attempt to control the diminutive aspects of a task or assignment.

S-DAD-CAI Model - The 7 emotional reactions employees experience when confronting what they deem to be calamitous change. The steps of the model include:

Shock **D**enial **A**nger **D**epression **C**ompromise **A**cquiescence **I**ntegration

Super-Templates - Cognitive shortcuts to aid in processing the immense volume of data we are exposed to in an incredibly short period of time. In essence, the super-templates allow for form of pattern recognition.

Unconscious bias - Unconscious bias refers to assumptions and conclusions formulated outside of our conscious awareness.

Made in the USA
Monee, IL
26 February 2022

91901234R00118